m9410953

15·99

Rethinking Special Needs in
Mainstream Schools
Towards the Year 2000

Rethinking Special Needs in Mainstream Schools Towards the Year 2000

Edited by

Alan Dyson and Charles Gains

David Fulton Publishers
London

David Fulton Publishers Ltd
2 Barbon Close, London WC1N 3JX

First published in Great Britain by
David Fulton Publishers 1993

Note: The right of the contributors to be identified as the authors of their
chapters has been asserted by them in accordance with the Copyright, Designs
and Patents Act 1988.

British Library Cataloguing in Publication Data

A catalogue record for this book is available from the British Library

ISBN 1–85346–221–7

Typeset by Action Typesetting Limited, Gloucester
Printed in Great Britain by BPCC Wheatons Ltd, Exeter

Contents

vi

Contributors

Tony Booth Senior Lecturer in Education in the School of Education, the Open University.

Catherine Clark Lecturer in Education in the School of Education, University of Newcastle upon Tyne.

Alan Dyson Lecturer in Education (Special Educational Needs) in the School of Education, University of Newcastle upon Tyne.

Patrick Easen Lecturer in Education in the School of Education, University of Newcastle upon Tyne.

Roy Evans Assistant Dean of Education (INSET), Roehampton Institute of Higher Education, London.

Norah Frederickson Associate Tutor in Educational Psychology, University College London and Senior Educational Psychologist, Buckinghamshire LEA.

Charles Gains Editor, *Support for Learning* (a journal of the National Association for Special Educational Needs).

Ian Galletley Principal, Oakfield Vocational College, Newcastle upon Tyne.

Jean Luscombe Head of Learning Skills, Cirencester Deer Park School, Gloucestershire.

Donald McIntyre Reader in Education, Department of Educational Studies, University of Oxford.

John Moore Senior Phase Inspector for Special Educational Needs, Kent LEA.

Colin Nash Research Fellow, Institute of Continuing and Professional Education, University of Sussex.

Christine O'Hanlon Lecturer in Education (Educational Psychology and Special Educational Needs) in the School of Education, University of Birmingham.

Elizabeth Scott Special Needs Development Officer, Cheshire LEA.

Janet Simpson Senior Teacher (Learning Support), William Howard School, Brampton, Cumbria.

David Thomas Senior Lecturer in Education and Head of the In-Service Unit in the Department of Education, University of Liverpool.

Introduction

A book such as this, like the elephant, takes about 18 months to gestate. It generally starts with a feeling of dissatisfaction about current trends and events and a desire to discover if these views are shared by others. Contributors are sought who share this unease. The hope, pious though it may be, is that the collection of thoughts and opinion will 'gel' into an important advance in the chosen field. Recommendations are made to that end.

Little could the editors have anticipated the enormous amount of change that would take place in just a year and a half. Two ambitious Secretaries of State, neatly divided by a General Election, and the consequent mountain of legislation and instruction, have thrown an already depressed profession into further turmoil. The White Paper, *Choice and Diversity*, has set down directions for the remainder of the decade that will be received with enormous trepidation by those committed to the alleviation of learning difficulty and underachievement. All this is accompanied by a frenzied, and at times ill-informed, debate about standards in education. At the time of writing economic developments within the European context threaten further disruption and confusion.

There has been little opportunity to reflect in such frenetic times so it is interesting to return to the original premises that prompted this excursion into print. Briefly, these were as follows:

- There remain incompatible elements between the 1981 Education Act and the 1988 Education Reform Act that have yet to be resolved.
- A strong suspicion is emerging that the integration of pupils has largely been carried out in a hasty and disorganized fashion.
- Statementing of pupils, regarded as a panacea by some, has come under criticism for its largely anodyne nature and,

further, fails remotely to address the massive problems of underachievement that still exist in our school system.

- Existing and proposed legislation is highly likely to undermine, if not destroy, the fragile services that have evolved over decades to protect those at risk.
- Special educational needs, always a messy area, is lurching into further trouble lacking an agreed definition, a coherent strategy and clarification of new roles.
- Devolved budgets and rampant market forces will marginalize those with special needs. They are, virtually by definition, 'losers' before the first ball is kicked.

These, and other arguments, propelled us in a certain direction in the Spring of 1991. However, constant discusssion revealed yet another facet of the debate. We became convinced that there was an underground shift of opinion, of seismic proportions, that had been in train long before Government interference. It appeared that the liberal ideology that had underpinned developments since World War Two, had run its allotted course. Enormous achievements had, of course, been made in its name but, despite this attitude and provision, still remained firmly locked into the child deficit model. Special educational need was trapped and searching for a way out.

The Warnock Report of 1978 briefly raised hopes of a transition from one era to another. Much was made of the integration of pupils with difficulties into mainstream situations but the debate largely centred on logistical concerns rather then serious educational advancement. It is unsurprising that serious doubts have surfaced about the speed at which this was implemented.

By the late 80s the focus had shifted from improved provision to simple survival. Pragmatism was in danger of overcoming compassion; reasoned debate had gone underground. It was in this climate that we invited a collection of experienced and talented individuals to contribute to a book. There is little we need say as an introduction; the chapter headings speak for themselves. The reader may find it useful to make a concerted effort and study all the inputs. Alternatively, and more probably he, or she, will want to dip at random into these substantial offerings. Whatever path is chosen, we trust this will help all those who are genuinely concerned about the future of special educational needs.

Finally, it seems appropriate that as a result of this venture we should attempt to summarize one or two of our thoughts:

- The term 'special' has always been misleading and a search for its replacement must surely be undertaken. We have in this decade to address some huge difficulties and will need to direct the attention of decision makers away from the 'wheelchair syndrome'.
- We can view with some pride the achievements of the past but it is not helpful to dwell on these and hope for a return to more charitable and easy going times. We need to focus objectively on the opportunities that present themselves.
- We share with colleagues the fears of competitive models Government is anxious to introduce and believe that collaborative strategies offer more promising routes.
- We offer in the final chapter an example of such a strategy. Clusters and consortia of schools and institutions are emerging to meet particular needs and circumstances. To date these remain local, spontaneous and loosely structured. We hope the model profferred will prove useful in understanding this approach, focusing discussion and exploring possibilities.

We would like to thank all of our contributors. They have substantially altered our perspectives. We trust they will do the same for the reader.

Alan Dyson
Charles Gains
1993

CHAPTER 1

Using Soft Systems Methodology to Re-think Special Needs

Norah Frederickson

Many of the contributors to this book suggest that there is a need to re-think special educational needs. This chapter addresses the practical issue of *how* we should go about this rethink. It is first of all argued that, however we go about it, our approach should be systematic and explicit. The second part of the chapter introduces one approach – Soft Systems Methodology (SSM) – which appears particularly suited to conducting an action-orientated rethink of special needs in mainstream schools. The final section outlines ways in which SSM has been used by groups and individuals in schools and Local Education Authorities to reflect on practice and effect improvement.

Special needs: a complex mess?

It may appear unnecessary to dwell on the assertion that any rethink of special needs should be conducted in a systematic and explicit manner. It might be accepted as obvious and uncontroversial in this era of accountability. However it is not the way in which change has typically been designed and managed in educational contexts. Indeed words such as 'designed' and 'managed' are part of a new vocabulary which appears to fit uneasily with talk of 'philosophy' and 'good primary practice'. Dyson's (1990) comments about the 'whole school approach' to special educational needs could as easily have been directed at any number of educational practices brought to the fore by the pendular swings of fashion, 'the approach as a whole seems to have found its way into educational practice without any sort of rigorous evaluation and there is little or nothing in the literature about how it has been or might be evaluated.'

There are, of course, well developed and highly respected methods for conducting rigorous evaluation, within the scientific tradition, and it is perhaps not surprising that authors engaged in debate on special needs have urged the use of empirical data and experimental trials, 'from which one could make generalizations according to the canons of scientific research' (Kauffman 1989). However, schools have little in common with well controlled laboratories and repeatable experiments, in human science contexts, are difficult to achieve as Checkland and Scholes (1990) point out. Nonetheless, there has been extensive application of scientifically based ideas to the field of special needs by the various professionals involved whose activities are well described by Schon (1983) in his critique of the 'technical rationality' view of professional activity: 'professional activity consists in instrumental problem solving made rigorous by the application of scientific theory and technique'. This is well illustrated by the prominence of scientifically based problem solving approaches in educational psychology over the past decade (Cameron and Stratford 1987, Frederickson, Webster and Wright 1991). While acknowledging the existence of 'high, hard ground where practitioners can make effective use of research-based theory and technique', he argues that practitioners may more often find themselves in a swamp where many of the problems of greatest human concern exist as, 'confusing "messes" incapable of technical solution.' Soft Systems Methodology has been developed as an organized way of tackling messy situations in the real world. It provides an intellectual framework based on systems thinking which allows a practitioner, operating in an action research mode, to make sense both of the situation and of their involvement in it. In education and social science generally the label 'action research' is applied to much wallowing around in real world messes. Checkland and Scholes (1990) lament that discussions of action research, 'on the whole unfortunately neglect the crucial importance of declaring the intellectual framework' as 'it is with reference to the declared framework that "lessons" can be defined.' (p.16).

A major contributing factor to the 'messiness' of many problematic situations and issues in education is substantive differences in the perceptions and intentions of those involved. In these cases it is not possible to embark on a classical problem solving approach because it is not possible to agree on a definition of *the* problem or achieve consensus on the objectives of any change. In these situations there is a need for an explicit approach which can represent the range of views held without requiring that they be reconciled in order for progress to be made. This is likely to be particularly important in the field of special needs as the current US debate over the Regular Education Initiative (REI) illustrates. There is a number of illuminating parallels between the REI debate and the 'Dyson Debate' (Dyson 1990, Butt 1991) on the future role of the special needs co-ordinator in UK schools, however, the following brief discussion will focus on those aspects which illustrate the need for an approach which can accommodate a range of conflicting views.

The Regular Education Initiative is an umbrella term for a set of proposals for radical restructuring of special and general education in the US. At its core is the, not unfamiliar, view that education for pupils with special needs will be best served by the improvement of education for all pupils. It is further elaborated by Kauffman (1989), one of its main opponents, as requiring that:

> Students of every description are fully integrated into regular classes, no student is given a special designation (label), costs are lowered by the elimination of special budget and administrative categories, the focus becomes excellence for all, and federal regulations are withdrawn in favour of local control (p.256).

Proponents of the Regular Education Initiative (McLeskey, Skiba & Wilcox, 1990) are critical of the current fragmented approach to pupils with special needs and are concerned about the stigmatization of pupils on 'pull out' (withdrawal) programmes. They argue, along similar lines to Booth (1986), that values rather than data should determine social policy. 'Data can be used to evaluate progress towards the goals established by values, but data cannot alter the value itself' (McLeskey, Skiba & Wilcox, 1990, p.322). They therefore point to the right of all children, under Public Law 94–142, to a free appropriate education in the least restrictive environment as central.

Opponents of the Regular Education Initiative (Kauffman, 1989) criticize its proponents for naïvety on two accounts. They first of all argue that a mainstream classroom may not be the least restrictive environment for all children, and indeed that the objective of providing appropriate education should take precedence over that relating to the setting in which it is provided. Secondly they demonstrate that the Regular Education Initiative can be perceived as being underpinned by a quite different set of values from those espoused by its proponents. Hence Kauffman (1989) argues:

> The belief systems represented by the REI are a peculiar case in which conservative ideology (focus on excellence, federal disengagement) and liberal rhetoric (non-labelling, integration) are combined to support the diminution or dissolution of a support system for handicapped students.

The critique of Kauffman's paper by Goetz & Sailor (1990) in which they paraphrase him thus, 'REI is a Regan – Bush plot to cut the costs of special education' (p.335) will sound familiar in the context of UK debates on integration and in-class support strategies.

Kauffman characterizes proponents and opponents of the Regular Education Initiative as espousing an opposing set of assumptions or beliefs:

Proponents hold that:	*While opponents believe that*:
Pupils are more alike than different. The same basic principles apply to learning of all, so no *special* teaching is needed by any.	Some pupils are very different from most and special educational approaches are required to meet their needs.
Good teachers can teach all pupils, using the same basic techniques but making some adjustments for individual differences.	Not all teachers are equipped to teach all pupils, special expertise is required to teach pupils with special needs who are particularly difficult to teach.
All pupils can be provided with a high quality education without identifying some as different and targeting funding separately.	Pupils with specials needs must be clearly identified to ensure that they receive appropriate services.
All pupils can be taught and managed effectively in the mainstream classroom, segregation of pupils with special needs in any way is ethically unacceptable.	Education outside the mainstream classroom is sometimes required for part of the school day to: (a) provide more intensive individualized instruction, (b) provide instruction in skills already mastered or not needed by most pupils, (c) ensure the appropriate education of the other pupils.

Attention has also been drawn to the impact of these different sets of beliefs on the UK debate on the future role of special needs co-ordinators. Dyson (1990) argues that the 'whole school approach' is founded on assumptions, 'that special needs children learn in much the same way as all other children, and that the so-called expertise of special needs teachers can in fact be spread amongst subject and class teachers' (p.118).

The above discussion demonstrates that the field of special educational needs is characterized by a diversity of approaches, underpinned by conflicting beliefs and riven by disagreement about fundamental issues — such as how special educational needs should be defined. It would appear to be well characterized as one of Schon's (1983) 'confusing messes' and, in its rethinking, to require an approach which can bring systematic, logical analysis to bear without oversimplifying the real complexities of the situations studied or underestimating the impact of human perceptions and interests in effecting or resisting change.

Soft Systems Methodology

Soft Systems Methodology (SSM) is an approach which can be used to guide intervention in the kinds of ill-structured, real world problem situations common in the field of special needs. Checkland, who is Professor of Systems and Information at the University of Lancaster, developed the methodology through a programme of over 100 action research consultancies in commercial and service environments, including health and social service contexts (Checkland 1981, Checkland and Scholes 1990). Soft Systems Methodology adopts a positive approach which is sensitive to context. It does not focus on the problem but on the situation in which there is perceived to be a problem, or an opportunity for improvement. The initial task is not to converge on a definition of a problem to solve, but to build up the richest possible picture of the situation in question, drawing on the disparate perceptions of those involved.

The essential nature of SSM is summarized in Figure 1. In overview, it consists of some stages where you engage in finding out about and developing a representation of reality, some stages where you develop a model of a system which might be relevant to changing/improving reality and, finally, some stages where you draw comparisons between your model and your representation of

Figure 1

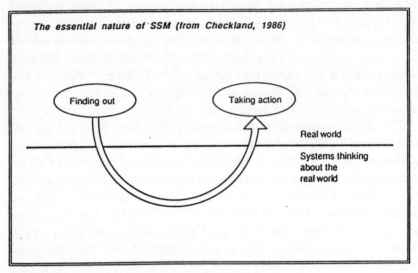

The essential nature of SSM (from Checkland, 1986)

reality in order to generate improvement suggestions/recommen-
dations for action.

For descriptive purposes SSM consists of the seven stages which
are represented diagrammatically in Figure 2.

In Stages 1 and 2 you would be involved in finding out about a
particular problem situation, collecting information and identifying
important themes and issues. You may collect information by a
number of different means, for example, interviewing, observation.
These are practical activities where you will need to do something
in the real world.

In Stages 3 and 4 you would use aspects of systems theory to
analyse the problem situation and to build models of systems which
may be relevant to improving it. Notice the words used. A model
relevant to improving a problem situation does not purport to be
a model of a problem/or a problem situation. These activities are
purely logical/theoretical. A more detailed discussion of different
strands of systems theory and their application in schools can be
found in Frederickson (1990a).

In Stages 5 to 7 you would be involved in suggesting
possible changes to the real world situation whose desirability and feasibility those directly involved could debate
and, if appropriate, implement. (The last three stages again
involve practical activities, such as meetings and feasibility

Figure 2

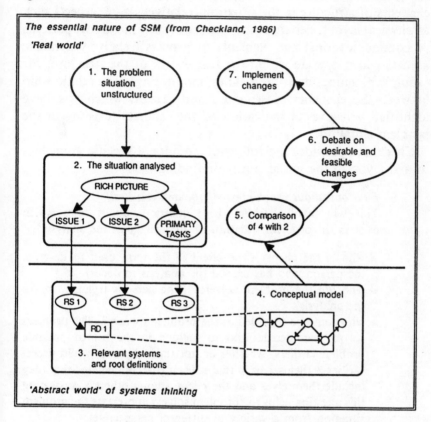

The essential nature of SSM (from Checkland, 1986)

studies which would need to be carried out in the real world.)

You will notice the distinction which is drawn between Stages 3 and 4, the below line stages, and the other five stages, the above line stages. Stages 3 and 4 are theoretical in that they involve formal systems thinking whereas the other five stages are practical in that they involve activities which are carried out in the real world.

The seven stages of Soft Systems Methodology are now described in more detail.

Stage 1. The problem situation: unstructured

The task in Stage 1 is to find out about the problem situation while trying not to impose a particular structure on it. Checkland suggests a number of things which it might be useful to find out about the problem situation. He suggests that you attempt to identify elements of structure in the situation (relatively static aspects such as physical layout, departmental structure, staff hierarchy, patterns of communications) and elements of process (relatively dynamic aspects which operate within the framework of the structure, for example planning, decision making, monitoring). The relationship between the elements of structure and process which you have identified will give an indication of the 'climate' existing in the problem situation.

Checkland provides the following additional specific guidelines to assist you in the initial stages of finding out:

1. *Find out about the context of the analysis itself*
   This will involve asking three questions about roles which exist in the problem situation as a corollary of the analysis:

   - who is the client? (The client is the term used to describe the person who has caused the analysis to occur)
   - who are the problem solvers? (The persons trying to make the analysis)
   - who could be regarded as the problem owners? (The problem solvers can decide who to include in the list of possible problem owners, whether or not those persons would necessarily see themselves in that role. It is recommended that they include themselves and the client among others.) Answering this question helps the problem solvers appreciate the problem situation from a variety of different perspectives.

2. *Find out about the social aspects of the situation*
   Find out about the norms, roles and values which exist in the situation. What roles (formal or informal social positions) are accepted, what behaviour is expected in them and how is performance judged? Why is Sue Brown regarded as a good class teacher or a weak headteacher or a supportive colleague? What do you have to do to get on in All Souls High School?

3. *Find out about the political aspects of the situation*
   What are the sources or commodities of power in this situation? (They may have to do with access to or control of certain information or people, the ability to set up structures, long involvement with the organization, role in the organization and external recognition) How are such commodities obtained, preserved, passed on, for example?

Stage 2. The problem situation: expressed

The information obtained is used in Stage 2 to express, represent or describe the problem situation – to build up the richest possible picture of the situation. This may be a pen picture but it is often found to be more useful to express the information diagrammatically or indeed pictorially.

A rich picture is defined as an evolving diagram which collects together and portrays key information and impressions about a complex situation in a loosely structured and evocative way. Such a picture is likely to contain patterns or aspects which the problem solvers regard as significant in some way or encapsulate particular features of the situation – these can be selected as problem themes. Such a picture is also usually capable of being viewed from a variety of different perspectives. At Stage 3 consideration of these different viewpoints and problem themes will allow the problem solvers to select a number of particular systems which they hypothesize to be relevant to debate about the problem situation with a view to bringing about improvement. Figure 3 contains an example of a rich picture (of the operation of a Local Authority secondary support base for 'vulnerable' pupils) where the emphasis is on the structural and procedural aspects of the problem situation. Figure 4, on the other hand, contains an example of a rich picture (of the problem situation faced by a group of staff charged with the production of a curriculum five year plan for their school) where the social and political aspects of the situation are evocatively expressed.

Stage 3. Relevant systems and root definitions

At Stage 3 then the problem solvers attempt to analyse the situation systematically by taking the view points/issues identified at Stage 2 and naming a number of notional systems which may be of relevance (Relevant Systems). For example, Naughton (1984) suggests that either of the following systems might be considered relevant if the problem situation were an English pub:

> an alcohol retailing system
> a system for initiating adolescents into the adult culture.

He identifies the first as a fairly obvious example of a primary-task system whereas the latter is a rather unexpected example of an

Figure 3

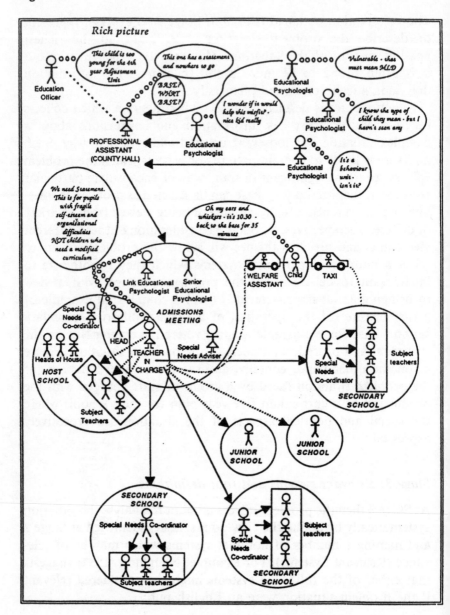

Figure 4

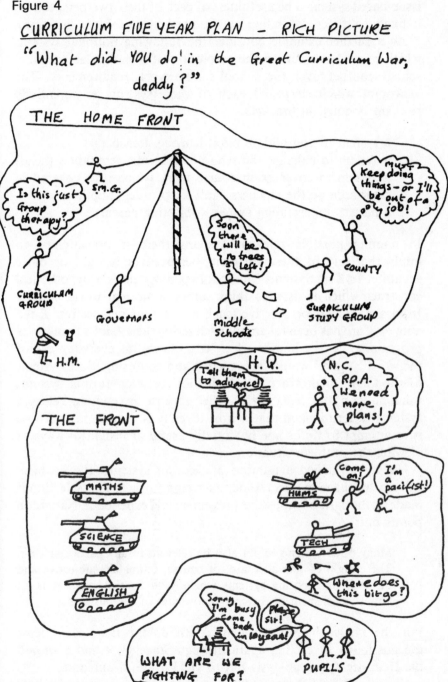

issue-based system. The usefulness of each of these two perspectives is likely to differ depending on the particular problem situation.

As a further example consider the following notional systems which proved relevant to the resolution of a particular parent – school conflict over the school's homework requirements. The viewpoint which suggested each of these systems as potentially relevant is noted in brackets.

> a system to consolidate pupil learning (teachers)
> a system to enhance the school's academic reputation (head)
> a system to cover exam course work which isn't covered in class because the teachers can't keep order (pupil)
> a parent undermining system (objecting parent)

In naming possible relevant systems there is no attempt to imply that any of these different perspectives is right or more accurate. In Soft Systems Methodology a system is a hypothetical construct which is used to think about some real world activity from a particular perspective (such as the four perspectives listed above). Care has been taken not to describe the school's homework programme as 'the homework system' since this everyday use of the word 'system' would be incorrect and confusing. Soft Systems Methodology makes a clear distinction between formal systems thinking and the real world. The purpose in naming relevant systems is not to claim that is how it really is. Rather the purpose is to attempt to find some potentially useful or insightful ways of viewing the problem situation.

Having identified a number of relevant systems, the problem solvers then have to select some to develop further. This selection is made on the basis of subjective judgement and experience. Naughton points out:

> Many other systems might also be relevant to any particular case. The criteria of relevance are, of course, ultimately subjective and the skill of choosing systems which yield fruitful analyses is an important element in the craft knowledge of the business.

For the novice in Soft Systems Methodology there is at least the possibility of cycling again through Stages 3, 4 and 5 should the first attempt at analysis fail to yield a useful outcome.

Checkland and Scholes (1990) state that an important aim of Soft Systems Methodology is, 'to take seriously the subjectivity which is then the crucial characteristic of human affairs and to treat this subjectivity, if not exactly scientifically, at least in a way characterized by intellectual rigour' (p.30). The rest of Stage 3 and Stage 4 therefore involve the logical development of the Relevant Systems which have been selected. The relevant systems are first defined more clearly. This is done through producing a root definition of each, which describes its basic nature in a way designed to be revealing to those in the situation. The value of root definitions is not judged in terms of their correctness, but in terms of their usefulness in illuminating ways in which aspects of the problem situation can be helpfully changed.

To provide a clear definition of the system under consideration, the root definition should contain the following six elements:-

C – Customers (victims or beneficiaries of the system)
A – Actors (who carry out the activities of the system)
T – Transformation process (what the system does to its inputs to turn them into outputs)
W – *Weltanshauung* (the view of the world that makes this system meaningful)
O – Owner (who could abolish this system)
E – Environmental constraints (what in the environment this system takes as given).

Here is an illustration which is taken from a worked example on in-service training provision for special needs which was generated by Peter Checkland during an advanced professional training course for educational psychologists and senior secondary teachers held at University College London in July 1988. One of the Relevant Systems selected was: a system to provide special needs in-service training for mainstream teachers. The following CATWOE analysis was produced:

C – mainstream teachers
A – those who do in-service training
T – need to cope with Special Needs in mainstream >T> need met by in-service training
W – desirable/possible to educate special needs pupils in mainstream
O – headteacher
E – 1981 Education Act, resources available, school culture and structure

The associated Root Definition was: A headteacher-owned system, staffed by INSET trainers which, given the constraints of the 1981 Education Act, available resources and the school structure and culture, provides to selected teachers that INSET which is deemed necessary to enable them to cope with pupils having special educational needs in mainstream lessons.

The transformation process is at the heart of the root definition. It should be noted that the input to the transformation process must be present in the output although in a changed form; in the example given the input is a need and the output is that need met.

Stage 4. Building conceptual models

The root definition describes what the system *is*. In order to describe what it *does* it is necessary to build an activity model of the system. This model will be conceptual in that the problem solvers must strive to make it a purely logical representation of the activities which would necessarily have to happen in the system described by the root definition. No attempt should be made either to model what really happens or what might ideally happen. Your model is only a relevant intellectual construct to be used to help structure debate. At this stage comments are often made about the advantages of having included among the problem solvers an 'outsider' whose greater distance from the real world situation helps to retain an appropriate focus on the logical and conceptual nature of the model building.

The crucial components of the model will be activities, represented on paper as verbs. The task is to assemble in correct order the minimum number of activities required in the operation of the human activity system described by the root definition. The aim is to have between six and twelve main activities. These may subsequently be broken into sets of subsidiary activities as necessary. Conceptual models may be constructed as follows:

- write down verbs associated with obtaining input
- write down verbs associated with the transformation
- write down verbs associated with dealing with output
- arrange the list of verbs into a logical sequence, connect verbs with arrows which indicate logical dependencies

- to the structured set of verbs comprising the operations of the system add a control system of the general form:

i)   define criteria for measure of performance
ii) monitor operations
iii) take control action

In considering the issue of evaluation Checkland argues that five different aspects need to be considered: efficacy, efficiency, effectiveness, ethicality and elegance (the last two of these having recently been added to the first three, Checkland and Scholes, 1990). In evaluating efficacy one needs to ask whether the system is in fact functioning, whether the transformation is being carried out, whether the means selected works. In evaluating efficiency one needs to ask whether the system is operating with minimum resources, including time. The evaluation of effectiveness involves asking whether the transformation at the heart of the system is the right activity to be doing in the first place. You should notice that questions about effectiveness can only be answered from outside the system in question, by reference to larger systems of which it is a part. Considerations of ethicality require us to consider whether the transformation is a moral thing to do, while the evaluation of elegance would focus on the extent to which the transformation is aesthetically pleasing.

The conceptual model shown in Figure 5 was developed from the root definition in Checkland's worked example which was described above.

It is important to note that conceptual models describe *what* must be done rather than *how* it is to be done. The example in Figure 5 includes 'decide who shall provide INSET' as a stage in the model. There is no indication how this decision should be made, but a clear indication of what should precede it (a decision about what INSET is needed).

Stage 5. Comparison

At Stage 5 the conceptual models which have been produced during Stage 4 are compared with the real world (the problem situations expressed in Stage 2). This comparison may reveal mismatches:

- are some logically necessary stages simply left out of the process which operates in real life?

Figure 5

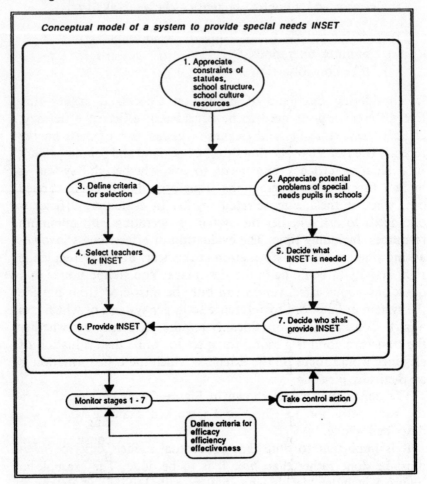

Conceptual model of a system to provide special needs INSET

- is operational effectiveness being reduced by the inclusion of unnecessary stages?
- are activities happening in an illogical order?
- are the activities being performed well?

Stage 6. Debate on feasible and desirable changes

The identification of mismatches at Stage 5 is used at Stage 6 to structure a debate among those who inhabit the problem situation about possible changes which could improve the situation. Checkland and Scholes (1990) emphasize that consensus is only occasionally likely to be achievable. In general the aim will be to achieve an accommodation between different interests, 'in which the conflicts endemic in human affairs are still there, but are subsumed in an accommodation which different parties are prepared to go along with'. The debate aims at identifying changes which meet two criteria; the changes must by systemically desirable, as indicated by the conceptual modelling activity and they must be culturally feasible, given the characteristics of the situation and the people in it. Note that in the real world it may be desirable to move the real situation futher away from that expressed in the model. For example, a model of a prison as a system to train criminals might well relevant, but the Home Office would hardly wish to make it more so!

Stage 7. Action to improve the situation

Stage 7 involves the implementation of the changes which have been agreed. This may be straightforward or it may generate other difficulties which can in turn be tackled using the methodology in further cycles.

Although the methodology has been described in stage by stage sequence, in the interests of clarity of exposition, Checkland emphasizes that much iteration between stages is expected and indeed desirable. For example, in selecting relevant systems at Stage 3 it may well be useful to test out various possibilities by quickly looking ahead to Stages 4, 5 and 6 and seeing what kind of models might follow from the root definitions considered and what kinds of changes are likely to be generated in the comparison stage. Also, Stage 5 almost always leads to more finding out being thought necessary.

Checkland points out that the methodology should not be regarded as a once-and-for-all approach to something sharply defined as a problem but as a general way of carrying out purposeful activity which gains from the power of some formal systems thinking but at the same time does not require individual human beings to behave as if they were rational automata. Hence the methodology deals with fuzzy real world messes, whereas many alternative approaches require clearly defined problems/objectives. Such 'hard' approaches also typically produce ideal systems, modelled by experts, which are imposed on the situation and the people within it as solutions. Soft Systems Methodology, by contrast, produces systemically desirable and culturally feasible changes to the existing situation, these changes having been selected by those who live in the situation.

However democratic this sounds it must be acknowledged that inequalities of power in the existing social order can be expected to influence the debate. (It would be a brave probationary teacher who persisted in arguing against the headteacher's point of view.) In criticism, therefore, it could be argued that SSM merely facilities a social process in which essential elements of *status quo* are reproduced. This will depend on the way in which it is used. As a cyclic learning process the methodology as described is essentially neutral. Any use of it will not be. It will be radical or reactionary depending on the user and the situational constraints. In this respect the explicitness built into SSM is particularly valuable. Anyone nominating a potentially relevant system must be prepared to state the *weltanshauung* underlying it.

Dyson (1990), for example, speculates that special needs co-ordinators may only continue to be employed with the advent of financial delegation if they can demonstrate their cost-effectiveness. It is perfectly possible, using Soft Systems Methodology, to work through, 'a system to maximise the cost-effectiveness of special needs co-ordinators to their schools'; but not without explicitly stating the *weltanshauung* underlying it – which may be something like 'a school's most important task is to balance its budget'. Following this scenario through to its logical conclusion would result in a very different vision of the future for special needs co-ordinators than that portrayed by Dyson (1990) or Butt (1991) – a group of legal eagles, totally *au fait* with all the legislation circulars of guidance and case law relating to pupils with special needs. Through producing exquisitely documented cases they will seek to attract to their school the maximum possible allocation of Local Management of Schools (LMS) special factor funding and maximise the numbers of pupils receiving additional funding through statements. (Advice and assistance to parents on requesting an assessment under the Education Act 1981, and on formulating an appeal to the Secretary of State should their request be refused, may be a related activity.) Another strand of work might entail setting up and managing the paperwork associated with the alternative educational programmes to run from March to August in Years 9 and 11 to accommodate those pupils for whom General Directions under Section 19 of the Education Reform Act provide a convenient means by which the school's published assessment results can present the best possible picture in the open enrolment market place.

This example is intended to illustrate graphically the way in which Soft Systems Methodology can assist in suspending preconceptions and allowing a range of possible purposes to be logically worked through, future scenarios constructed, their implications systematically identified and their cultural feasibility openly debated. Although it is more common to model relevant systems which most participants regard positively, much can also be learned from exploring familiar issues from an unfamiliar perspective – one school quickly instituted new procedures after discovering how closely a model of 'a system to discourage poor attenders from coming into school' matched their present approach! Modelling scenarios which are regarded as potentially threatening and undesirable may help to identify ways in which they can be averted just as modelling culturally feasible scenarios should help to identify positive action which will effect improvement.

Applications of Soft Systems Methodology in schools

Prior to the 1988 course in Soft Systems Methodology at University College London taught by Peter Checkland only one unpublished master's dissertation recorded an attempt to apply SSM in a school. Following the course a booklet of the resulting studies with a foreword by Checkland was published (Frederickson, 1990b). The studies differ considerably in terms of the amount of time devoted to them and the level within the organization at which issues were addressed: individual pupil, classroom, department, heads of faculty, senior management team, whole school, cross school project team, local education authority working group. The studies also differed greatly in terms of the problem situations on which they focused, although the predominance of educational psychologists and special needs staff involved resulted in a high representation of special needs issues:

- the operation of support teaching in a secondary school containing integrated provision for physically handicapped pupils
- the provision of whole school in-service training in behaviour management at primary level
- facilitating the operation of local education authority working group on 'disaffected pupils' and quickly pulling together a coherent set of recommendations

- providing a framework to guide the work of a secondary school's behaviour project team in helping four recently amalgamated schools review their rules and routines
- assisting heads of learning in a secondary school to review their work, identifying and implementing desired changes
- offering an approach to school self-review in a secondary school concerned to address the question, 'the average child, the silent majority, could we be doing more for them?'

The booklet also contains a number of accounts where the methodology is used by individual practitioners to think through some aspect of their work in a coherent way; a teacher describes an analysis of a successful change in classroom layout while an educational psychologist describes an application in a school-based consultation about an individual child.

Finally the booklet contains one account of the kind of consultancy work using Soft Systems Methodology which is now offered by the Educational Psychology Group at University College London. It describes an application of SSM as a framework for evaluating a new local authority provision — a secondary support base for 'vulnerable' pupils. Anyone who is planning to become involved in school inspections would be well advised to give thought to the desirability of basing their work on a systematic and explicit approach, just as schools will be well advised to hold such teams to account in providing justification for the questions asked, the evidence collected and the conclusions drawn.

The authors of the accounts in the booklet record difficulties encountered as well as successes achieved, problems experienced with aspects of the methodology as well as positive aspects of its use. Overall there emerges a view that SSM is a useful approach in tackling constructively the fuzziness and complexity of many problems currently facing schools. It is to be hoped that it will prove of value to practitioners engaged in the task of rethinking special needs.

References

Booth, T. (1986) 'Is integrating the handicapped psychologically defensible?' *Bulletin of The British Psychological Society.* **39**, 141.

Butt, N. (1991) 'A role for the SEN co-ordinator in the 1990s: a reply to Dyson', *Support for Learning.* **6**(1), 9–14.

Cameron, R.J. and Stratford, R.J. (1987) 'A problem-centred approach to the delivery of applied psychological services'. *Educational Psychology in Practice* **2**(4), 10–20.

Checkland, P.B. (1981) *Systems Thinking, Systems Practice*. London: Wiley.

Checkland, P.B. (1986) *A Basic Introduction to Systems Thinking*. Unpublished paper, University of Lancaster.

Checkland, P.B. and Scholes, J. (1990) *Soft Systems Methodology in Action*. London: Wiley

Dyson, A. (1990), 'Effective learning consultancy: a future role for special needs co-ordinators?' *Support for Learning* 5(3), 16–127.

Frederickson, N. (1990a) 'Systems work in EP practice: A re-evaluation', in Jones, N. and Frederickson, N. (Eds) *Refocusing Educational Psychology*. London: Falmer Press.

Frederickson, N. (ed.) (1990b) *Soft Systems Methodology: Practical Applications in Work with Schools*. Educational Psychology Publishing: University College London.

Frederickson, N., Webster, A. and Wright, A. (1991) 'Psychological assessment: A change of emphasis, *Educational Psychology in Practice* 7(1), 20–29.

Goetz, L. and Sailor, W. (1990) 'Much ado about babies, murky bathwater and trickle-down politics: a reply to Kauffman', *The Journal of Special Education*, 24(3), 334–339.

Kauffman, J.M. (1989) 'The Regular Education Initiative as Regan–Bush education policy: a trickle-down theory of education of the hard to teach,' *The Journal of Special Education*, 23(3), 256–278.

McLeskey, J., Skiba, R. and Wilcox, B. (1990) 'Reform and special education: a mainstream perspective,' *The Journal of Special Education*, 24(3), 319–325.

Naughton, J. (1984) 'Soft Systems Analysis: an introductory guide', in *Complexity, Management and Change: Applying a Systems Approach. Open University Course T301, Block IV*. Milton Keynes: Open University Press.

Schon, D.A. (1983) *The Reflective Practitioner: How Professionals Think in Action*. London: Temple Smith.

CHAPTER 2

Special Needs and Standard Provision

Donald McIntyre

The 1981 Education Act defines children with special needs as those with 'a learning difficulty which calls for special educational provision to be made'. It also explains that 'special educational provision' should be taken to mean 'educational provision which is additional to, or otherwise different from, the educational provision made generally for children of his or her age in schools maintained by the local education authority concerned'. Thus the Act wisely recognized that the specialness of 'special needs' is not in the children concerned but in the provision to be made. All children, it rightly implied, have distinctive needs and all, in some contexts, at some times, and for some learning, having learning difficulties. Any system designed for the education of a whole population is, however, necessarily based on the premise that, through its standard means of provision, the system can and does adequately provide for the needs and difficulties of the great majority of members of the population. Equally, however, any system, and any standard provision have limitations; and it is the limitations of the system's standard provision which lead to a need for special provision for needs and difficulties not catered for by the standard provision.

In this paper I shall try to examine some of the characteristics of the standard provision which is currently made available. In particular, I shall seek to consider what aspects of this standard provision would have to be changed in order for it to meet the needs of a substantial proportion of children for whom special provision is currently necessary.

The standard provision made for children's education in Britain, and in most other countries, is **classroom teaching**, characterized typically by the collection of twenty to forty pupils in one room with a single adult teacher, and in most cases by the treatment of this collection of pupils for at least some of the time as a single social group. It is true of course that the alternative types of provision, such as open-plan schools, team-teaching, and the use of resource-centres for independent learning, are also well established; but the main provision made for the great majority of the school population continues to be classroom teaching.

As Hamilton (1986) has reminded us, classroom teaching is a fairly recent invention:

> As an architectural unit, the classroom came to prominence in Britain after the 1830s with the gradual spread of state-supported (and state-supervised) schooling. By the 20th century, the batch-production rhetoric of the classroom system (for example lessons, subjects, timetables, grading, standardization, streaming) had become so pervasive that it successfully achieved a normative status – creating the standards against which all subsequent educational innovations come to be judged. Indeed, the widespread penetration of the classroom system had another important ideological effect. It obscured the fact that, before about 1800, schooling had been organized around a quite different vocabulary, and quite different assumptions, resources and practices (ibid, p.68).

Viewing educational practice as being shaped by the interacting effects of economic realities and the history of ideas, Hamilton persuasively represents the classroom system as a response to the social changes, the felt social and economic needs, and the dominant metaphors and ideas associated with the industrial revolution. He also raises the question of why the classroom system (eventually) flourished in preference to the much cheaper monitorial system of Bell and Lancaster; and he suggests that this happened because the classroom system was informed by ideas which were powerfully influential in the early nineteenth century: the importance of **emulation** as a motivating force; the rationalist concern with **intellectual** growth; and the belief that such growth could best be facilitated by flexible **teacher – pupil interaction** which combined the advantages of simultaneous instruction with those stemming from a teacher's knowledge of individual pupils.

Classroom teaching, construed in such terms, was always an ambitious enterprise: the teacher accepts obligations not only to manage the classroom group so as to make membership of it beneficial to all its members, but also to take account in his or her teaching of the attainments and learning difficulties of each individual. I shall argue both that during the last 150 years the task has become even more ambitious and complex, and that such an ambitious and complex task has been undertaken successfully only through the adoption of well tuned strategies for simplifying it.

In the meantime, we should attend to Hamilton's message that classroom teaching, our current standard provision, is far from an inevitable fact of nature. On the contrary, it was developed to meet the needs, and within the frame of thinking, of the new industrialized societies of the nineteenth century; we should be ready to entertain the possibility that it is not the most appropriate form of standard provision to serve post-industrial societies.

Classroom teaching and students' different learning needs

In order to consider how far and in what ways it might be useful to modify our current standard provision so as to cater for a wider range of pupils' needs and difficulties, it may be helpful to ask how adequately it caters for the range of needs and difficulties which are not at present generally viewed as special.

There are, of course, different kinds of classroom teaching systems. They may conveniently be dichotomised into those in which the classroom teaching aims to look after the full range of pupils' learning needs (except perhaps some special needs) and those in which pupils are allocated to different classes according to their differing levels of academic attainments of abilities. The latter category encompasses considerable variety in relation to the criteria and procedures for differentiating among pupils, the number of differentiated groups, and the specificity of purpose for which the differentiation is made. However, it does seem unlikely that **any** such differentiated system is likely to offer a useful starting point for reconstructing standard provision so as to provide for pupils currently seen as having 'special' needs. Any such widening of the scope of standard provision is more likely to start from existing systems committed to meeting heterogeneous needs rather than from those which depend on homogeneity within classes. It is therefore appropriate to ask how successful classroom teaching has been when it has sought to meet a wide heterogeneity of needs; in other words, how effective has mixed-ability teaching been?

Twenty years ago, we had good reason to believe that a move towards mixed ability classes would produce substantial benefits:

the undesirable effects of ability grouping of classes had been clearly demonstrated. The rigidity of such grouping and the expectation effects it fostered seemed clear from studies such as those of Jackson (1964), Douglas (1964) and Douglas, Ross and Simpson (1968); and the polarization of school populations into pro-school and anti-school sub-cultural groups which seemed to follow from streaming (eg. Hargreaves, 1967; Lacey, 1970) made the task of teaching many classes hopeless and compulsory school attendance futile for many. The large-scale National Foundation for Educational Research (NFER) study in primary schools (Barker-Lunn, 1970) suggested that mixed-ability teaching would produce positive results if only the teachers involved were committed to it.

Given these well-founded hopes of twenty years ago, it is disappointing to have to recognize today that neither common experience nor systematic research has demonstrated that mixed ability classrooms have generally led to improvements in pupils' educational attainments (Slavin, 1987a, 1990a). The Banbury study (Newbold, 1977; Postlethwaite and Denton, 1978) has been fairly typical in demonstrating that mixed ability class grouping has substantial social benefits and that in general it has no disadvantages in relation to educational attainments; but nor does it generally foster higher educational attainments. Perhaps surprisingly, research findings indicate that mixed ability teaching does not even have advantages or disadvantages for the more able or the less able pupils.

What such research does not tell us is why mixed ability classrooms have been so disappointing in their effects on educational attainments; for that we have to look elsewhere. Studies of teachers' experiences of mixed ability teaching (e.g. Reid et al, 1981) have found that teachers frequently report that classroom management is more difficult in mixed ability classrooms and that they find it difficult to cater for all ability groups. Her Majesty's Inspectorate have written, especially in a 1978 report, of the inadequacy with which many teachers match the tasks they set to the differing abilities of their pupils. Two research studies (Bennett et al., 1984; Simpson, 1989) have examined this claim in relation to primary school teaching. In both studies it was found that teachers differentiated among pupils in the tasks they gave them, with the pupils experiencing tasks as being of the type intended by teachers in about 80 per cent of cases. However, for certain kinds of task and certain kinds of pupil, the matching was much less satisfactory. In particular, for more able pupils:

> Teachers could indicate that something new was about to be introduced, whereas our observations indicated that on half of these occasions the pupils already knew it, or had had experience of it, and were therefore practising it. Similarly, one third of the tasks intended to offer enrichment were experienced as straightforward practice skills. (Simpson, 1989, p.11)

As a separate exercise, the researchers in both studies themselves judged, on the basis of pupils' performances, whether or not the tasks set were matched to their individual knowledge and skills. They judged that approximately half of all tasks were well matched to the pupils' needs, and concluded also that there were strong tendencies for teachers to overestimate the capabilities of children whom they themselves saw as less able and to underestimate the capabilities of those they saw as more able. The same trends were apparent in both studies.

These studies therefore give considerable support to the HMI view that pupils' differing needs are frequently not catered for in mixed ability classrooms. A strong implication of this must be that the standard provision made for pupils' learning needs in such classes would **not** be at all appropriate provision for children whose learning difficulties are judged to be more severe or more distinctive than those of the pupils currently being taught in such classrooms.

These studies also go some way towards explaining why mixed ability classrooms have not done more to improve children's educational attainments. Indeed, they go further, through having sought the teachers' perspectives. Simpson, for example, reported her findings back to the participating teachers who, it should be noted, had been invited to participate because their employers nominated them as good and experienced teachers. The teachers agreed that the trends reported for over and underestimation were probably a fair reflection of children's experience in their classrooms, and in addition raised the following points:

(i) there were limits to the number of different groups or distinctive individuals with which they could cope at any one time

(ii) having a wide spread of ability in their classes was greatly preferable in the interests of both teachers and children to grouping children into classes according to ability

(iii) whereas the study had been concerned only with pupils' 'academic' needs, it was also important to cater for their diverse social and emotional needs

(iv) they deliberately gave special attention and extra resources to the lower ability pupils, because their need for teaching help was greater

(v) more able children in the classroom were a valuable resource in that they offered models of effective learning and problem-solving which could help the learning of other children

(vi) it was more useful for children's education to be broadened than for them to 'shoot ahead' of their peers; however the provision of breadth depended on the availability of appropriate resources and of time

(vii) while the research had concentrated on number and language tasks, it was also necessary to provide a wide curriculum

(viii) if children appeared to be over-practising it was almost certainly related to the teachers' concern to ensure that the basic skills had been mastered; the teachers had to be mindful of prerequisites for the children's learning with the next teacher, the next stage of the curriculum, or the next school to which they were going.

This commentary by the teachers reveals something of the thoughtfulness and careful professional prioritization which underlies and to a substantial degree explains the observational findings. It also reveals something of the complexity of the work of classroom teaching.

Simplifying the complexity of classroom teaching

It has so far been suggested that since 'special needs' is properly defined in terms of standard provision, reconceptualization of special needs is likely to depend on the reformation of standard provision. It has been argued further that current standard provision, even in its most propitious form, systematically falls short of meeting the diverse needs even of those pupils for whom standard provision has been deemed to be sufficient. Finally it has been suggested that this may be understandable in terms of the thoughtful strategic judgements made by able, experienced, dedicated teachers faced by a highly complex task. In this section, the implications of this complex task will be further explored.

Classroom teachers depend upon many kinds of expertise, but the most essential and probably the least understood is that which is implicit in their own classroom activities and their orchestration of their pupils' classroom activities. This goes beyond their understanding of their pupils and their ability to relate to them, beyond their subject and curriculum understanding and the 'pedagogical content knowledge' through which they make subject knowledge accessible to pupils, and beyond their knowledge of the school and its way of doing things, although it depends on all of these. Terming this expertise of teachers their 'professional craft knowledge', Sally Brown and I have, in a recent study, (Brown and McIntyre 1992) tried to gain access to this expertise and to identify some of its common features. That there are common features is itself important because teachers, having largely developed their professional craft knowledge in the privacy of their own classrooms, inevitably vary widely in the specific things which they do and want in their classrooms. Several of the common features which we found are relevant to this present discussion.

We found that teachers, interviewed about specific lessons shortly after they had taught them, when asked what had gone well in the lessons, without exception talked about what the **pupils** had done. They had to dig much deeper to bring to the surface the things which they themselves had done which had facilitated these successes. Indeed they were almost always unable to recall the mental **processes** involved in deciding, their attention having been fully focused on external events. They were, however, able to talk about the particular actions they had taken in order to achieve their goals, and especially about the multiplicity of factors which they thought had influenced both their choice of action and the standard which they set. Among these factors were characteristics of individual pupils or of groups, time factors, content, resources, various aspects of context, and their self-perceptions. By careful probing we were able to bring to light some of the richness of the connections made between extensive repertoires of possible actions, drawn upon in the light of these multiple factors, but so fluently that an observer would not be aware of any decision being made. Indeed the decisions seemed to be generally more intuitive than made through rational deliberation: there would not have been time for the latter.

Even from this very general account, one important implication can be drawn. The intuitive fluency which characterizes such teachers' professional craft knowledge, and on which much of their success depends, can only be developed after several years of practice. It could not easily be replaced by new kinds of expertise of similar quality, and any successful attempt to replace it would have the initial effect of deskilling the teacher. Thus one could not expect, for example, that the introduction of another adult occasionally into such a teacher's classroom would lead to any significant change in their patterns of teaching; if it did, the change would probably be a disruptive one. For teachers to learn to take full advantage of such an arrangement, and to act with the fluency that they usually do on their own, would be a long-term achievement. This would be possible, and could well pay significant dividends, if such an arrangement were to become part of a new standard provision. So long as it remains something done occasionally to cater for special needs, it is unlikely to make a significant difference to the quality of teaching.

Another implication of the sophisticated fluency of teachers' professional craft knowledge is that it necessarily depends on taken-for-granted ways of conceptualizing classroom situations. Teachers learn ways of thinking about classrooms which they find useful and develop repertoires of ways of acting which depend on these ways of thinking. Concepts which simplify the situations to be dealt with in ways which relate to the choice of actions to be taken are especially valuable.

Probably the most important such simplifying concept for the most teachers is some variant of general ability, brightness or ability at the subject. The factors which were most commonly reported by teachers as influencing their choice of action were pupils' characteristics; and, as we have found previously (McIntyre and Brown, 1979) it was general ability which was much the most commonly mentioned characteristic.

It is worth dwelling on this point, since the majority of children with special needs are still widely seen as being appropriately and primarily categorized as being of low general ability. Also, as is apparent from studies reviewed above, Her Majesty's Inspectors and researchers find the concept equally convenient and acceptable. It is not difficult to understand why: not only is the concept crucial to the meritocratic ways of thinking about education which have dominated educational provision in this country throughout the twentieth century, it also provides a highly plausible and academically respectable way in which teachers can use a simple, stable and overarching framework with which to construe differences among pupils and so decide how to cater for them and how to use them in the classroom.

Yet it is a dangerously deluding concept. Denton and Postlethwaite (1985), investigating more able children in secondary schools, found that if the most able ten per cent were nominated in each academic subject, thirty-five per cent of the year-group would be mentioned. The same is true within subject-areas: ability to do one task well is a poor predictor of the ability to do other tasks well within the same subject curriculum (McIntyre and Brown, 1978). Thus this simplifying concept, which greatly facilitates the classroom teaching of most teachers, especially in mixed ability classes, seriously distorts teachers' attempts to meet the learning needs of their pupils. Indeed so long as teachers rely upon this concept, there is no possibility of them satisfactorily meeting the learning needs, or catering for the learning difficulties, of their pupils.

One striking feature of the professional craft knowledge of teachers (Brown and McIntyre, 1992) was the nature of the criteria in terms of which teachers assessed the success of their teaching. As previously indicated, these criteria without exception related to the activities of pupils. Most were expressed in terms of what we called 'normal desirable states of pupils' activity' – normal, that is, for particular kinds of, and stages of, lessons. Others were expressed in terms of 'progress' – the production of artefacts, the coverage of work, acting in ways more like the normal desirable ways or, occasionally, subject learning. In every case, however, these desired outcomes of teaching were **short-term** goals. Teachers, while engaged in their teaching, seemed not to be thinking in terms of long-term strategies but instead to be focusing on short-term goals which, presumably, they perceived to be conducive to the attainment of longer-term goals. This short-term perspective, which has been noted by other researchers (eg. Jackson, 1967) would seem to be another of the ways in which teachers simplify the complex task of classroom teaching. It too, however, must reduce the flexibility with which they plan to meet the learning needs of individual pupils.

Conclusion

Current standard provision, even at its best, is very far from successful in meeting the learning needs of all pupils for whose needs it is claimed to be satisfactory. Classroom teaching was a sophisticated and ambitious response to the historical need to develop a mass education system, and mixed ability teaching a fully justified version of classroom teaching appropriate for the provision of comprehensive primary and secondary education. Teachers have developed highly skilful and intelligently strategic approaches to the extremely complex task which mixed ability classroom teaching sets them, but these approaches are, on one hand, recognized as compromises and on the other involve tactics which greatly reduce the flexibility and sensitivity with which teachers can respond to individual needs.

The explicit premise of this paper has been that 'special needs' and 'standard provision' are different sides of the same coin. The implicit premise has been that a reformulation of both which better meets the needs of those pupils currently seen as having special needs will almost certainly be one which also better meets the needs of many for whom standard provision is currently seen to be adequate. That premise having been derived from a researcher's view of the educational world, it has been encouraging to read Dyson's (1992) account of the type of mainstream innovations which are occurring and which, as he writes, 'are applicable not just to pupils with special needs but to all pupils'.

It will be such practical initiatives which lead the way, but their cutting edge will be the sharper the more fully and clearly their theoretical assumptions are articulated. For me, there are four complementary theoretical perspectives which will all be important in reconceptualizing 'standard provision' and with it 'special needs'. These are:

(a) the place of the parent as primary educator and necessary partner for the teacher
(b) mastery learning, based on Bloom's (1977) argument that the variables affecting attainment are 'alterable'; argument still rages quite vigorously about the research evidence (e.g. Slavin, 1987b; Kulik, Kulik and Bangert-Drowns, 1990), but there seems little doubt that great things are **possible** through mastery learning

(c)   closer partnerships between teachers and learners, through supporting pupils as learning strategists (cf. Corno and Snow, 1986; Weinstein and Mayer (1986))

(d)   developing further the collaborative group-work long advocated by Kelly (1978) but perhaps with the slightly tougher focus on individual attainment articulated by Slavin (1990b).

References

Barker-Lunn, J.C. (1970) *Streaming in the Primary School*. London: NFER.

Bennett, N., Desforges, C., Cockburn, A. and Wilkinson, B. (1984) *The Quality of Pupil Learning Experiences*. London: Lawrence Erlbaum Associates.

Bloom, B.S. (1977) *Human Characteristics and School Learning*. New York: McGraw-Hill.

Brown, S. and McIntyre, D. (1992) *Making Sense of Teaching*. Milton Keynes: Open University Press.

Corno, L. and Snow, R.E. (1986) 'Adapting teaching to individual differences among learners' in M.C. Wittrock (ed.) *Handbook of Research on Teaching, Third Edition*. New York: Macmillan, 605–629.

Denton, C. and Postlethwaite, K. (1983) *Able Children: Identifying Them in the Classroom*. Windsor: NFER-Nelson.

Douglas, J.W.B. (1964) *The Home and the School*. London: McGibbon and Kee.

Douglas, J.W.B., Ross, J.M. and Simpson, H.R. (1968) *All Our Future*. London: Peter Davies.

Dyson, A. (1992) 'Innovatory mainstream practice: what's happening in schools' provision for special needs?' *Support for Learning*, 7, 2, 51–57.

Hamilton, D. (1986) 'Adam Smith and the moral economy of the classroom system', in P.H. Taylor (ed.) *Recent Developments in Curriculum Studies*. Windsor: NFER-Nelson, 84–111.

Hargreaves, D. (1967) *Social Relations in a Secondary School*. London: Routledge and Kegan Paul.

Her Majesty's Inspectorate (1978) *Mixed Ability Work in Comprehensive Schools*. London: HMSO

Jackson, B. (1964) *Streaming: An Education System in Miniature*. London: Routledge and Kegan Paul.

Jackson, P. (1968) *Life in Classrooms*. New York: Holt, Reinehart and Winston.

Kelly, A.V. (1978) *Mixed Ability Grouping: Theory and Practice*. London: Harper and Row.

Kulik, C.C., Kulik, J.A. and Bangert-Drowns, R.L. (1990) 'Effectiveness of mastery learning programmes: a meta-analysis', *Review of Educational Research*, **60**, 2, 265–299.

Lacey, C. (1970) *Hightown Grammar: The School as a Social System*. Manchester: Manchester University Press.

McIntyre, D. and Brown, S. (1978) 'The conceptualization of attainment', *British Education Research Journal*, **4**, 2, 41–50.

McIntyre, D. and Brown, S. (1979) 'Science teachers' implementation of two intended innovations', *Scottish Educational Review*, 11, 1, 42–57.

Newbold, D. (1977) *Ability Grouping: The Banbury Enquiry*. Slough: NFER.

Postlethwaite, K. and Denton, C. (1978) *Streams for the Future?* Slough: NFER.

Reid, M., Clumies-Ross, L., Goacher, B. and Vile, C. (1981) *Mixed Ability Teaching: Problems and Possibilities*. Windsor: NFER-Nelson.

Simpson, M. (1989) *A Study of Differentiation and Learning in Schools*. Aberdeen: Northern College.

Slavin, R.E. (1987a) 'Ability grouping and student achievement in elementary schools: a best-evidence synthesis,' *Review of Educational Research*, **57**, 3, 293–336.

Slavin, R.E. (1987b) 'Mastery learning reconsidered', *Review of Educational Research*, **57**, 2, 175–214.

Slavin, R.E. (1990a) 'Achievement effects of ability grouping in secondary schools: a best-evidence synthesis', *Review of Educational Research*, **60**, 3, 471–500.

Slavin, R.E. (1990b) *Co-operative Learning: Theory, Research and Practice*. Englewood Cliffs, NJ: Prentice-Hall.

Weinstein, C.F. and Mayer R.F. (1986) 'The teaching of learning strategies' in M.J. Wittrock (Ed.) *Handbook of Research on Teaching, Third Edition*, New York: Macmillan, 315–327.

CHAPTER 3

Turning the Kaleidoscope: Working With Teachers Concerned About Special Educational Needs

Catherine Clark and Patrick Easen

Education, it might be argued, is about

- the achievement of understanding (for it is this that distinguishes 'education' from 'indoctrination'); and
- a concern to foster 'open minds' rather than minds that are 'closed'. (This is *not* a distinction between having or not having commitment to or firm belief in something rather than a comment on the way those beliefs are seen. A closed mind accords beliefs the status of unquestionable truths, open minds do not).

Clearly, if this is the case, then it raises questions about both what it is that should be understood and how this understanding should be brought about. Even in the age of the National Currciulum teaching is, or at least should be, concerned with those questions ... and none more so than in relation to 'special needs'.

Learning and the *learner*, we would argue, need to be at the heart of any attempt to answer those questions. At the moment the focus of much of the educational debate is on *instruction* and *management* whether we are talking about pupils or teachers. In keeping with our title, then, this chapter looks at the same phenomena of underachievement from this different position. It is a shift that is both crucial and, possibly, revolutionary given the *zeitgeist* of late twentieth century Britain. We suggest this for two reasons. First of all, if those concerned with education really were to focus on *children's learning* and study cognition before considering how teachers and schools should service its needs and requirements then many classrooms and schools would need to be stood on their heads. (Of course, that may not be a bad place to stand some of them!) Secondly, if the realization were to dawn that educational change is about *teachers' learning* – as individuals and collectively – then it would be seen, in Fullan's (1991) words 'as a process not an event' . . . and a complex process at that.

We recognize that the following discussion is both oversimplified and limited. Learning itself is complex and cannot easily be considered separately from the person who is the learner. There is not one type of learning but several. Nor is there one process of learning (in the sense of a set of steps which is applicable for each and every particular act of learning) but many. Furthermore, viewing classroom teaching processes as actions that directly foster learning may be an incomplete way of conceptualizing teacher action. 'Learning', for the large part, takes place in the social context of the classroom where 'order' has to be created and sustained. 'Order' requires a teacher to establish structures and procedures for handling the group processes of the classroom so that the acceptable limits of various aspects of pupil activity are defined and controlled. Some types of learning may create pressures on the order system and a teacher may experience tensions and dilemmas arising from the two tasks of 'maximising learning' and 'sustaining order'.

Given all these caveats, however, we wish to question some of the ways in which special needs are currently defined and then handled. A more promising approach, we suggest, is to consider special needs in the more general context of problems relating to teaching and learning in classrooms. This may entail a fundamental reconceptualization of teaching and learning; representing, in turn, a major challenge for professional development and the ways in which it may be supported.

'Seeing' the problem of underachievement in the classroom

Classrooms are busy places and, by their nature, make impossible demands upon both the children and teachers within them. One way in which teachers simplify the situation and make sense of it is to operate with implicit norms both for events and for children. In this way 'problems' arise and are subjected to 'conscious processing' when those norms are not met. Often this happens when particular children present learning and/or behavioural difficulties. This is evidenced in statements such as:

- (s)he can't concentrate
- (s)he is easily distracted
- (s)he lacks motivation
- (s)he doesn't know how to behave
- (s)he doesn't want to learn
- his/her communication skills are poor
- (s)he has no language

Typical responses by teachers regarding ways in which such children can best be helped tend to stress the need for increased provision of people (especially those with expertise in the field), time and materials. Whilst it is indeed possible that resources might alleviate some of the difficulties of both children and teachers, it is a truism that resources are finite. This is particularly so at the moment in an economic and political climate where funding is increasingly tied to specific initiatives and underpinned by an ideology which demands easily indentifiable and measurable outcomes.

Such children as those described above are often defined as having 'special needs' and present their teachers with problems which often persist despite careful and committed efforts to remediate the situation. Even when that additional resourcing is made available and intensive help is provided on an individual basis by a specialist support teacher, the apparent gains are rarely sustained. In the final analysis, then, despite the burgeoning knowledge and expertise that exists in relation to special needs, improvements in pupil learning remain elusive. Naturally this is a cause for concern for both teachers and parents; particularly given the heightened expectations post-Warnock and the 1981 Act.

Usually the approach for handling these pupils is based upon a rather technical model of teaching and learning with, in effect, the presenting needs being fed into the equivalent of a 'what to do when things aren't working' algorithm. Teachers with expertise in this field have become skilled diagnosticians who provide explanations as to why a child is not learning to read, able to spell and so on. In fact a great deal of time has been spent in identifying who has special needs and in undertaking detailed assessments of performance for those identified. Indeed it is not uncommon for both specialist special needs teachers and class teachers to claim that they do more testing than teaching.

Defining as 'seeing'

We would suggest, however, that these very notions are them-selves problematic. For example, presenting 'needs' may well be symptoms rather than causes of problems; simplistic 'diagnostic' approaches may neglect the complex nature of the person who constitutes the particular learner; and everyone may have 'special needs' at particular times in particular contexts. As Goacher et al (1988) showed, 'special educational needs'; is a relative term and dependent upon so many variables that, in effect, it becomes fairly meaningless in generic usage. What, then, does this mean for the practising teacher?

Wagner (1987) uses the term 'knot' to describe an internal affective conflict experienced by a teacher when (s)he perceives a violation of 'known truths'. As these 'understandings' are unquestionable, then a teacher finds difficulty in coping with events or situations which may render them problematic but in which (s)he cannot conceive of alternative interpretations or actions. We would argue that, for many teachers, particular children who present learning or behavioural difficulties represent 'knots' in relation to their classroom teaching. On this basis, then, the problems of handling children with special needs are nested within more general problems of handling teaching and learning in the classroom. They present differences of emphasis rather than of kind and, in doing so, their difficulties of understanding and of commitment are more visible. We would conclude with Edwards and Mercer (1987) that:

> 'learning failures' are not necessarily attributable to individual children or teachers, but to the inadequacies of the referential framework within which education takes place. In other words, they are failures of context. (p.167)

Perhaps cutting the Gordian knot of 'special needs' can only be done through a consideration of this wider context.

Bennett et al (1984) show that even in classrooms which teachers would describe as 'child-centred' the actual experience for the children was likely to be teacher dominated and in essence, traditional. This kind of learning, especially for children described as having special needs, is almost *de rigueur*. In order to release the stranglehold of this orthodoxy, the National Curriculum Council, in its guidance to teachers of children with special needs (1989), advocates a three step process for learning and teaching which moves from highly structured learning to independent learning. So often special needs teaching, with its emphasis on the passive role of the learner, and its insistence on breaking down learning into small, linear steps, such as in precision teaching, remains locked into the first of these three steps. Not only do teachers organize the learning experiences for special needs children in this way, but both Delamont (1987) and Alexander (1984) describe many primary classrooms in which the learning experience for all children is prescribed to a great extent by the teacher. If such classrooms are, indeed, commonplace then it implies that significant professional development may be involved when special needs issues are being considered. But how this is to be done may require some major rethinking about what is involved in professional development.

We believe that two of the key issues concern the concepts of 'typification' and of 'routinization'. Given the nature of classroom teaching it is inevitable that teachers categorize events. Indeed Doyle (1986) suggests that successful teachers engage actively in the cognitive processing of information during teaching. In particular, this involves 'rapid judgement', 'chunking' (grouping discrete events into larger categories) and 'differentiation' (sifting in terms such as 'of immediate or of long-term significance' or as 'important or incidental'). Small wonder, then, that teachers also categorize pupils. Such typifications are often informal but that does not detract from their power. 'Types' not only help a teacher to impose meaning or 'sense' on complexity, they also shape what (s)he sees or believes about his/her world and become a basis for action within it. Typifications facilitate classroom teaching by enabling 'routinization'; once typified, pupils can be worked on with routines established as appropriate for their category (appropriateness, of course, being a function of the teacher's belief and value systems). This raises questions about the suitability both of a teacher's typification for individual pupils and of his or her routines for handling particular 'types'. Such questions, however, strike at the very heart of professional knowledge; teachers pride themselves on 'knowing' their pupils and regard the fostering of learning as their specific professional skill.

Classrooms as characterizations of implicit assumptions

Analysing classroom practice in terms of typifications, routines and the underlying assumptions about teaching and learning is, we believe, helpful. Many classrooms are managed on a daily basis in ways that strive for the individualization of both learning and teaching. For special needs children this may be carried to its logical conclusion in the withdrawal of children from normal classroom activities to engage in concentrated teaching of 'basics' (often related to language development or the teaching of reading). Without wishing to parody such classrooms it is possible to construct characterizations of their norms as in Figure 1. In effect, we could claim that such classrooms are based on a behaviourist or 'transmission' model of teaching and learning.

Figure 1: A characterization of the classroom based upon behaviourist assumptions about learning

UNDERLYING TEACHER ASSUMPTION	ACCOMPANYING TEACHING ROUTINE
• learning is an individual process	• children work as individuals
• learning results from the activity of the teacher	• one-to-one teaching whenever possible
	• child's access to the curriculum is mediated by another (preferably a suitably qualified teacher)
• learning is a cognitive activity	• decontextualized learning activities
• knowledge is both sequential and hierarchical	• provision of a restricted curriculum (because some aspects are more important than others)
	• highly structured programme of learning activities
	• demands of 'match' necessitate restricted autonomy

It would appear, however, that other models of teaching and learning — and in particular constructivism — have much to offer as a way of understanding learning difficulties and, therefore, of handling special needs. A constructivist view of learning is based on the premise that while knowledge is intrinsically social and cultural, its starting points are essentially subjective and individual. It is constructed by the learner through activity in the physical environment and through social interaction in which discussion and communication enables sense to be made of those experiences. Thus classrooms based upon this premise are likely to provide the child with maximum flexibility to learn in a way that is meaningful to him or her. As such there will be opportunities for collaborative learning and an emphasis upon the teacher as 'scaffolder'. A characterization of the norms of such a classroom might be as in Figure 2.

Teacher development as seeing different configurations of the 'known'

Space precludes any detailed discussion of the relative merits of behaviourist, constructivist or even rationalist theories of learning as the basis of classroom models for teaching. Suffice it to say that any unexamined assumptions which underpin practice in a classroom will limit the possibilities for developing the repertoire of that classroom ... and teacher learning must be at the heart of that. Furthermore, our view of teaching as characterized by typification and routine presents an interesting issue concerning teacher learning. One thing it suggests is that significant professional development is more to do with what teachers *do* 'know' rather than with what they *don't* 'know'. In other words, rather than learning more, teachers may need to learn about the same things but in ways that enable them to find different configurations for their existing knowledge. Of course for this to happen they have to be aware of what they know and that may mean gaining access to the vast stores of undifferentiated events and implicit theory that constitutes their personal professional knowledge. Only then can they seek to develop more sophisticated and complex typifications as a basis for action in the classroom.

Identifying those aspects of teacher thinking and the concomitant classroom practice to be developed, however, is not

UNDERLYING TEACHER ASSUMPTION	ACCOMPANYING TEACHING ROUTINE
• learning is both an individual and a social process	• children have opportunities to work both collectively and on their own
• learning results from the activity of the learner through interaction with experiences and with other people (not just a teacher)	• children are meaningfully engaged with their learning experiences
	• 'special needs' children can be integrated into classroom experiences
• learning is a holistic activity with conative and affective dimensions as well as the cognitive	• learning activities are embedded in a context that is meaningful to the learner
	• provision of a wide, rich and varied range of learning opportunities
• knowledge structures are more like complex networks than simple ladders	• the growth of knowledge is scaffolded during the learning rather than pre-ordained in the planning
	• children have autonomy in their learning activities

Figure 2: A characterization of the classroom based upon constructivist assumptions about learning

the same thing as establishing any new practice as a norm in the classroom. As we have noted, one of the biggest factors to be taken into account in any attempt to facilitate these developments is the taken-for-granted assumptions and common sense used by teachers to interpret their classroom experience. So, for example, the contexts created for learning by a teacher together with how (s)he handles a learner's responses within that context will be determined not only by how that teacher typifies the learner but also by whatever assumptions (s)he holds about how learning takes place. There is, in fact, a matrix of assumptions within which classroom practice is nested; this includes assumptions not just about children but also about how they learn, the nature of knowledge, what teaching involves and so on. All of these assumptions contribute to helping a teacher make sense of or put meaning on what happens in the classroom. It amounts to what might be termed a 'meaning perspective' whereby the teacher sees and explains his or her classroom (including the activities of the pupils).

Perspectives, we would argue, are the key to understanding teacher development. Mezirow (1977), in the context of adult learning, crystallized transformatory learning as the process of perspective transformation. He saw it as the process whereby a person comes to look at his or her world (and thus give meaning to his or her experiences) in new and different ways. For teachers, Mezirow's ideas would involve:

- reflecting upon present practice, preferably in a systematic and rigorous manner
- acknowledging and questioning the assumptions underpinning that practice
- exploring other ways of interpreting what is happening (or might happen) in the classroom to get different perspectives or explanations of the experience and
- trying out or 'experimenting' with other perspectives (and their concomitant practices) until confident in using one that seems to 'make sense'.

The significance of this is that if the classroom practice of a teacher is to be transformed then the meaning perspective of that teacher has to be transformed. 'Meaning' we should add, implies both understanding (since a teacher cannot teach what s/he does not understand) and valuing (as probably a teacher will not teach what s/he does not value).

An obvious example of this process at work would be in relation to error responses in mathematics. Interpeted by a teacher as 'mistakes' these serve to indicate little more than an inability of the child to respond to teaching and, probably, a need for further practice; analysed in terms of systematic error strategies these offer access to the developing conceptual structure of the child and some guide to possible alternative actions on the part of the teacher. Through seeing things differently there is the possibility of thinking differently about the mathematical learning of that child and, as a consequence, to act differently in the classroom. Put like that, of course, the development of teacher behaviours and teacher perspectives seem rather straightforward, whereas in practice the interplay between them is more complex than the linear sequence of a listing suggests.

Supporting teacher development

Inevitably such a process tends to be not only challenging but also very discomforting and stressful. Most of us feel threatened by information and experiences that do not 'fit' with our normal way of doing (and thinking about) things. Anxiety during change is to be expected and, if not made manageable, can be the harbinger of tension, conflict and alienation − all rocks upon which many a proposed development has foundered. It is not something that can be removed from the development process, but there are practical things that can be done by the 'supporter' to make the development of new practice more effective. For example:

1. A starting point can be chosen for the development with which colleagues can identify but which contains within it the 'seeds' of the wider understandings to be developed. For example, looking at the mistakes children make in their mathematical calculations can be seen as having tangible benefits in the classroom but, in looking at how individual children might be helped, all the important messages about children learning mathematics are represented in a practical form. As the strategies are worked in the classroom they start to become meaningful to the teachers.

2. Find ways to encourage the exploration, clarification and making sense of existing practices and value systems, otherwise the limitations of these may not be realized and no inherent reason to develop will be evident. There are a number of ways of collecting actual evidence of pupil activity and learning and those used do not need to be complex. Indeed, complex checklists and category systems for observing classroom life can be both inappropriate and inhibiting. Brief observations of individual pupils, conversations with them about their perceptions of their work or a collection of photographs taken to illustrate some aspects of classroom life can be rich sources for subsequent analysis. Ten minutes of pupil activity can encapsulate a vast set of educational principles to be considered.

44

Figure 3: Encouraging a cycle of action and reflection

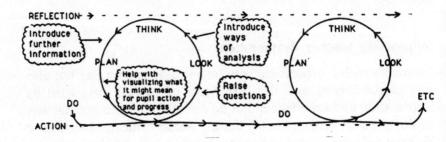

3. Encourage a regular cycle of action and reflection within the development and vary input to the cycle accordingly. Thus, there are times when it is appropriate to stimulate awareness, others when it is appropriate to introduce new information, yet others when help with skills practice may be most appropriate. Figure 3 illustrates how this might be done. This pattern of trying things out, seeing what happens, seeking explanations and planning further steps helps to move those involved from feeling confused and reactive in their situation towards being critically aware of and feeling more in control of it.

4. Help those involved to visualize what the new practice looks like in operation. Part of the difficulty of changing practice is that past 'measures' of pupil progress may no longer be adequate but teachers may be unsure of what might replace them. Consequently teachers do not really know quite what to look for in the new practice so they have no real way of deciding how well they are doing – apart, that is, from less than satisfactory 'indicators' from previous experience. This makes the task of adequate explanation and, perhaps justification, to others such as parents even more difficult. The generation of appropriate classroom descriptions of the sorts of things children do when engaged in appropriate learning and the ways in which they show signs of progress under the new practice is relatively simple and, when done collaboratively, helps to build shared visions of and value systems for the new practice.

Effective developments in classrooms and schools, we suspect, tend to be 'practice-led' but that does not mean that they are atheoretical. All practice contains within it theory of some form or other. Teachers inevitably will have developed their own set of ideas or theories about the practice of teaching even if they do not realize it. Implicit and personal as such theories might be, they become the touchstone for the intuitive actions within the classroom which shape the actual curriculum as experienced by the learners. As such they can become powerful inhibitors of professional development. Creating new norms of practice is not about attempting to stop someone from doing something (if, in legal or moral terms, there is a case for stopping a practice then that is a management problem rather than a professional development issue). Rather it is about helping them to increase their repertoire of ways of thinking about and handling their professional activities. This means finding ways of helping those teachers involved to bring to the surface those implicit theories with their associated assumptions and values so that they are able to reflect on, reframe and explore their own and others' interpretations of practice. In effect, it involves helping them to realize that there are feasible choices open to them and that these may be acted upon in the classroom. Starting with the actions and statements of teachers and the meanings that they currently put upon these does not mean that the work ends there, it just happens to be a way in which new ideas may be given an opportunity to take root. Whether they flourish or not depends to a large extent on the support structures available or created. Routinization is a part of being an expert since it involves the efficient and intuitive use of acquired skills. Moving to a new meaning perspective, however, means moving from being an 'expert' to being a 'novice' again ... and novices need the careful and detailed support of good 'scaffolding'.

Transforming the metaphor

It seems to be commonplace these days to talk about putting teaching under the microscope. We would suggest, however, that probably this is not the most useful metaphor for some aspects of professional development. Instead we prefer to offer the metaphor of the kaleidoscope, for it seems to capture more completely the type of teacher-learning discussed in this chapter.

Through a kaleidoscope we see the same crystals but different patterns; we see what we have seen before but in ways that we have not, as yet, experienced: we lose a familiar pattern without knowing quite what new one will emerge. Each turn holds new possibilities as that which was invisible becomes visible.

This metaphor was not chosen lightly. Metaphors act to structure our understanding of a concept and its related activities. Perhaps, as a final thought, one further dimension of the metaphor deserves to be made explicit. It concerns perceived control of the 'turning'. We may have no control over the pattern that emerges, but we do have control over the initiation of that process of re-patterning by consenting to turn the kaleidoscope. As Common (1981) reminds us 'The real power in schools is the power of teacher consent'.

Significant professional learning may be, at times, a painful process but it is made easier by willing participation. At the end of the day no one can 'change' another person; the most that can be done is to provide a structure and the support which enables that person to change if (s)he chooses to do so. As Yingmin Xu (*Among Teachers Community*, Oct 1991, p.10) writes:

> You are always the one
> To turn the scope
> And interpret
> Your life.

References

Alexander, R. (1984) *Primary Teaching*. London: Holt, Rinehart and Winston.

Bennett, N. Desforges, C., Cockburn, A. and Wilkinson B. (1984) *The Quality of Pupil Learning Experiences*. London: L Eribaum Associates.

Common, D. (1981) 'Power: the missing concept in the dominant model of school change' in *Theory into Practice*, 22, 3, 203–209.

Delamont, S. (1987) *The Primary School Teacher*. Lewes: Falmer Press.

Doyle, W. (1986) 'Classroom organization and management,' in Wittrock, M. (ed) *Handbook of Research on Teaching*, (3rd Ed), London: Collier Macmillan.

Edwards, D. and Mercer, N. (1987) *Common Knowledge: the Development of Understanding*. London: Methuen.

Fullan, M. (1991) *The New Meaning of Educational Change*. London: Cassell Educational.

Goacher, B., Evans, J., Welton, J. and Weddell, K. (1988) *Policy and Provision for Special Educational Needs: Implementing the 1981 Educational Act*. London: Cassell.

Mezirow, J. (1977) 'Perspective transformation' in *Studies in Adult Education*, 19 (Oct) 153–64.

National Curriculum Council (1989) *Curriculum Guidance 2: A Curriculum for all*. York: NCC.

Wagner, A. (1987) "Knots" in teachers' thinking' in Calderhead, J. (ed) *Exploring Teachers' Thinking*. London: Cassell.

Yingmin Xu (1991) quoted in *Journal of Among Teachers Community*, No. 2 (Oct).

CHAPTER 4

Flexible Learning

Colin Nash

The convergence of the concept of flexible learning and special educational needs provision in mainstream schools focuses unambiguously on the needs of the individual learner.

When the research into the effective management of flexible learning in schools was set up at Sussex University in 1989 there was no particular emphasis placed on investigating the part played by special needs provision in secondary schools. The work of special needs, or learning support departments, was initially seen as no more or less important than the work of any curriculum subject area or organizational arrangements within the institution. An unintended consequence of the research, however, was the gradual discovery of the important role of learning support or special needs teachers in moving forward the kinds of development that the project had begun to define as fundamental to our understanding of 'flexible learning'. With hindsight it may seem unexceptional, indeed expected that this would be the case since those who work in mainstream special needs have, over a long period of time, developed particular expertise in designing and developing appropriate resources, working co-operatively with other teaching colleagues and above all responding to the particular needs of each individual student. That this was the case is highly significant to a growing *rapprochement* between special needs and all other provision within secondary schools. (I do not intend to imply that the general issues and implications do not apply to other sectors of education, only that our specific research territory was in secondary schools.)

The other side of the coin is the relevance of flexible learning to the concerns of special needs providers. The term 'flexible learning' is used here within the specific context of the Technical and Vocational Education Initiative's Flexible Learning Development.* In the early stages of the Development 'flexible learning' was treated as an umbrella term which included a wide range of innovations in the management of teaching and learning. The common ground was that they should fulfil two objectives:

1) to meet the learning needs of students as individuals and in groups through the flexible management and use of a range of learning activities, environments and resources and
2) to give students increasing responsibility for their own learning within a framework of appropriate support. (Eraut, Nash et al., 1991, p.11)

This twin focus on individual learning needs and responsibility for learning is entirely consonant with the prevailing wisdom in special educational needs. Wolfendale (1987) argues that the term, 'Special Educational Needs':

> ... must not be used to differentiate individual children from one another nor groups from one another. It has to be used, as it was intended (Warnock, 1978), to ensure a match between the learning needs at any one time of an individual child and the best provision and resources that can be made available for that child. (p.4)

Matching provision and resourcing with identified needs is surely the goal of all serious educators but the problem, as Wolfendale recognizes, is how to achieve this without labelling or classifying learners in a way that may undermine confidence and achievement. The notion of 'differentiation', now enshrined in the National Curriculum, was identified in the White Paper *Better Schools* (1985) since 'what is taught and how it is taught need to be matched to pupils' abilities and aptitudes.' This definition can be used to accommodate systems that segregate learners according to ability or 'special need'. But what has been observed from a flexible learning perspective is that the goal of matching teaching to ability and aptitude (leaving aside the contentious nature of these two terms) can only effectively be achieved through an identification of individual learning needs whether the learner is statemented, designated as having exceptional ability or one of the majority who are labelled as 'average'. Individual needs are not properly addressed by streaming or setting any more than by mixed ability classes that are taught by teacher-centred strategies.

Flexible learning is not the establishment of a new theory or 'school' but a bringing together of a diversity of concepts, experiences and practical developments which redefine learning as a process whereby students are able to become independent learners who can manage their own learning and determine their own goals. Consequently the teacher's role has to be extended and elaborated to facilitate a more flexible approach to learning. The renaming of established Remedial and Special Needs departments as Learning Support, Individual Needs, Support and Development signifies more than a cosmetic change. The new terms indicate the broadening of the scope of the 'clients' for such services, the change in field of operation for special needs teachers and the widening of their role to support other teachers as well as students.

The research at Sussex University on flexible learning sought to establish common elements in schools that were adopting the two aims outlined above. The evidence was that some degree of change was observed in the areas of teaching and learning styles, tutoring, recording achievement, learning resources, learning environment and external relations. These changes were affecting the organization of the school with particular repercussions for staff development, especially in relation to the management of learning. For change to have any lasting effect it had to be part of long term strategy and planning. At the heart of all this was a philosophy of education which put the student clearly at the centre of the learning process. It is an approach that requires planned support and development and affects all aspects of curriculum organization and management. One of the consequences must be a move from disparate departmental plans and policies which only relate to separate groups. Sayer (1987) makes it clear that any discussion of non-segregation:

> ... has to be about the needs of the whole population.... The organization is there to enable teaching and learning to take place. At the head must come, therefore, the delivery point of teaching and learning as a whole: the learning group and its general mentor, the tutor. (p.24)

It is significant that increasingly schools are defining a policy for learning but it is curious that this is only happening now, long after policy making for issues such as equal opportunities and anti-racism have become commonplace. Institutions are being driven to ask the naïve but central question: what is our primary purpose? There seems increasingly to be a common answer at least for special needs teachers as well as advocates of flexible learning. We now turn to some of the features observed during the project in the organization of teaching and learning which focus on meeting individual needs. There are three main areas: the interaction between teacher and learner; the management of resources; and the wider framework supporting the learning.

At the heart of this approach is the relationship between teacher and learner which is characterized as one of partnership. The managing role of the teacher is to assist the learner towards the ultimate goal of independence. Crucial to achieving this goal is the clear intention that learners must have responsibility for their own learning. This does not mean the abdication of the teacher. Equally the student can no longer just sit and hope the teacher will make it all happen but will become involved as a partner in the learning process. The setting of goals and targets from the outset of any course or study programme gives the learner an immediate sense of purpose as well as a reference point. While teachers have normally had the aims of a lesson worked out they have not always communicated their intentions to the students.

Teachers have usually tried to have a variety of materials for use in the classroom. What is less common is allowing the student to choose which particular resources to use. Some teachers find it hard to stop spoon-feeding and hand over such aspects of classroom management. But the project observed that the more responsibility the student has for the learning process the greater will be the sense of ownership.

This leads to the question of choice − not only choice of resources but between alternative activities and appropriate levels. The degree of choice will be controlled by external constraints, especially the requirements of the National Curriculum and examination syllabuses, but within these limitations the learner can still become much more identified with the process. The experience of teachers working within situations of greater student choice suggests that students are more able to make realistic assessments of their most appropriate level of working than is generally assumed. Anxieties (particularly parental) about whether or not children are being sufficiently 'stretched' are more likely to be met in a situation where the learner is involved in negotiating the outcomes of a specific learning activity because they have to accept responsibility and be fully involved in the task.

Another potential area of interaction between student and teacher is the assessment of performance. This is an appropriate development from the negotiation of tasks and learning outcomes.

To arrive at a shared or negotiated assessment will indicate a high level of understanding between learner and teacher. It is increasingly common also for teachers to encourage student evaluation of learning tasks or modules of work. If taken seriously such evaluations not only help the teacher in future planning but also enhance the students' sense of involvement.

Keeping careful records becomes even more important in classroom situations where students are working in a variety of ways, all at their own pace. Giving students responsibility for their own records will ensure that they have a clearer idea of their goals, their rate of progress and their actual levels of achievement. The sense of ownership is given tangible expression through a personal record book.

A further feature observed is that wherever possible there should be an active role for the student. This is based on a firm belief that most of the learning of concepts and skills occurs, not at first acquaintance, but during subsequent use. Proportionately far more effort is put into communicating new ideas to students than in helping them to put those ideas into use. This moves the notion of ownership from involvement in the process of learning to the acquisition of knowledge: not just memorization but the capacity to apply what has been learned to a variety of contexts and situations. In this sense, ownership becomes synonymous with learning. It is achievable when the needs of the learner are taken into account and the process is managed so as to enable learning through use.

To speak of a student-centred ethos in the nineties may be to run the risk of charges of being trendy and unconcerned with standards. Child-centred education has tended to have a bad press and although this has not generally been justified it is true that some of the approaches popular in schools in the sixties and seventies did lack rigour. Wolfendale (1987) proposes:

> ... a redefinition of child-centred education to take account of each child's learning needs, and acknowledge the 'special' nature of these, in so far as it become the collective responsibility of all in the school to ensure that these are met. (p.8)

If the flexible learning approach is adopted as a means of addressing seriously the needs of every individual child within a school then the keynote will be rigour both for learners (as indicated above) and for teachers (discussed later). However there is no need for coyness about the use of the term 'student-centred'. In the market-oriented climate in which education now operates it would be entirely acceptable to speak of being 'client-centred'. The pupils, students, learners are properly the clients in the business of education and if we do not put them centre stage then we obscure the proper purpose of our schools and other institutions of learning.

A striking feature of schools that have adopted flexible learning as central to their institutional development is the importance placed on a student-centred ethos. The grandest plans are of little use unless the action is underpinned by a philosophy that has been thrashed out by the main participants. It becomes the touchstone which is referred to regularly. The senior management play a critical role in ensuring that there is a shared understanding and commitment to change. While this is obviously true for carrying out any innovation, a policy which has a declared commitment to enable every individual learner to achieve leaves the staff nowhere to hide. The commitment to individual success is a powerful pressure to ensure that the system supports such achievement.

It also places a further demand on the institution's leaders to act with integrity. It is hardly appropriate for teachers to be advocating the principles of negotiation, collaboration, teamwork, independence and self-evaluation if they are not prepared to operate in similar modes among themselves. A management style is required that reflects these principles in the way that decisions are made and policy is formulated. Not only do students need to be empowered to cope with their own learning, teachers need to be empowered to know that their actions are not peripheral but central to the aims of the organization.

It has to be admitted that the majority of schools (or perhaps their senior management and governors) baulk at the prospect of the radical kinds of change that are implicit in taking flexible learning seriously. But it has also been observed that many teachers, some of many years standing, have been pleasantly surprised at the significant improvements in their students' attitudes and achievement which have resulted from adopting these approaches to learning. A fresh look at structures and procedures can give the opportunity to clear away the unnecessary deadwood of bureaucracy and to establish alternative systems based on openness and clear channels of communication. At a time when formal appraisal systems are being introduced, many teachers are sceptical and fearful about the way they will be used by 'management' to control and direct the work force. While such an approach is adopted by some managers in education it is out of sympathy with the predominant practice in industry of Human Resource Development. It is certainly out of sympathy with the approaches to organization and management implicit in flexible learning which are being implemented in an increasing number of schools and colleges.

One of the reasons that teachers hesitate over flexible learning is that they rightly divine that its adoption will mean significant changes in their own practice. The most effective catalyst in encouraging teachers to change has been when they have had the opportunity to observe or share with other teachers who are using flexible approaches. Fears that their role as teachers will be diminished are unfounded. To the contrary, their role is enhanced but also, at least initially, so is their workload. If adequate time could be given to preparation and training then many teachers would be persuaded to 'experiment'. Unfortunately the present climate is not conducive to the generous allocations made to in-service training only a decade or so ago. But the trend for home-grown INSET which capitalizes on in-house expertise brings us back to the link between flexible learning and special needs that was identified at the beginning of this chapter: the key role to be played by special needs teachers in flexible learning developments.

There are three distinct areas in which trained and experienced special needs teachers can contribute to flexible learning, particularly in respect of staff development: responding to individual student needs, collaborative teaching and design and development of resources. There is also the considerable expertise available in the literature from practitioners and researchers. Sayer (1987) rightly points out that:

> Much valuable thinking has gone into the curricular literature of special education; but its value would be greater if applied right across a system designed for the whole spectrum of individual needs. (p.95)

The function of special needs or learning support teachers in many schools has shifted from working exclusively with children to working predominantly with other teachers. Often this has meant not just being the expert but also sharing the chores: marking work and writing reports as well as 'supporting the main teacher as a human being.' The collaborative, team teaching style will enable the non-special needs teacher both to learn from the special needs teacher and also to maintain their status. The support teacher just coming into the class to help specific children has the double disadvantage of implying that the class teacher cannot cope and of unnecessarily focusing on the pupil with problems. In the team situation the load is shared, the support teacher is available to help any children in the class and is also able to apply diagnostic skills if involved over a regular period of time. This also links to the issue of developing appropriate learning materials. This may be best done as a result of observing specific individual needs and tailoring the materials to suit them.

More often than not the special needs teachers are those who have the most experience (and training) in curriculum development. Their skills can also be linked to wider provision of in-service training in the school on a range of issues: for example, specific teaching and learning strategies, individual counselling skills, diagnosis of specific learning difficulties, coping with emotional and behavioural problems, developing criterion-referenced learning objectives, appropriate language levels. It is not surprising that at one of the research schools the Support and Development Unit had a major function in determining quality control of the self-help materials prepared for the school's modular learning programme.

There is nothing sacrosanct about either the term 'flexible learning' or 'special educational needs' as was illustrated by the critic who told the project team that all we were really talking about was effective learning. We concurred except to point out that sometimes new labels are necessary to draw attention to the importance of the issues under consideration. Dyson (1992) in reporting the Innovatory Mainstream Practice project identifies schools who 'tend to find little use for the notion of "special needs" as usually understood' but which have a philosophy and practice which:

> ... seems to offer a genuine chance of giving all pupils access to an entitlement curriculum, and of offering support within that curriculum to all. (p.55).

What will be important for the next century is not the survival of provisional educational concepts but that future generations of learners will be:

56

... people who are flexible and adaptable, who can transfer
from one situation to another, who can apply their knowledge
and skills in a variety of contexts, who are equipped to work
in a high technology society, who will be able to communicate
effectively in Europe beyond 1992 and in a shrinking world that
increasingly has common problems to share. (Eraut, Nash et al.
1991, p.23).

Note

* The TVEI Flexible Learning Development had two main
strands: regional projects involved in actively promoting and
developing flexible learning strategies; and national projects,
such as the one carried out at Sussex University from 1989 to
1990, which fulfilled a supportive role through research and
development.

References

Department of Education and Science (1985) *Better Schools*. London: HMSO.
Department of Education and Science (1978) *Special Educational Needs (The Warnock Report)*. London: HMSO.
Employment Department (1991) *Flexible Learning: A Framework for Education and Training in the Skills Decade*. Sheffield: Employment Department.
Dyson, A. (1992) 'Innovatory mainstream practice: what's happening in schools' provision for special needs?' *Support for Learning* 7, 2, 51–57.
Eraut, M. Nash, C., Fielding, M. and Attard, P. (1991) *Flexible Learning in Schools*. London: Employment Department.
Sayer, J. (1987) *Secondary Schools for All? strategies for special needs*. London: Cassell.
Wolfendale, S. (1987) *Primary Schools and Special Needs: policy, planning and provision*. London: Cassell.

CHAPTER 5

The 'Youth Village'

Ian Galletley

Schools are not enough. They are part of life, even though they advise all of it. They provide the means by which certain parts of life are run, and they categorize and qualify children according to the values of contemporary society. They provide experiences and create capacities which can be applied, cashed in or enjoyed for their own sake. However, they never *become* life.

I once visited a youth village in another country. On admission the young people were as poor, and as challenging, and as tattooed as any at home. They liked the same things and reacted similarly to certain kinds of adult behaviour, but after a few months, things changed. Not only education was on offer, but also training, employment and housing. There was a completeness in the place, even though it was not all available to all the students all the time. What seemed to make a difference was the acknowledgement that these were the four key organizational needs of young people beyond the basic need for love and emotional security.

In recent years, the teaching for children with special needs has rarely been industrially or vocationally direct. It has concentrated on 'life' or 'social' skills, has emphasized the basic education of word and number and considered personality at length. Occasionally children have been able to make or mend something which was needed by someone else, but the link was rarely real, and the economics of such activities was at a very long arm's length.

Teachers of disaffected teenagers know that success often lies in getting them to do something, to make, create, earn, repair or renew. 'Success' in this case means a desire to do what is suggested, a cheerfulness and application whilst doing it, and a high quality of finished product or outcome.

Although these comments are proposed for teenagers who are retarded in their attainments, disinclined towards abstraction and often either absent from or difficult in school, bright children also suffer from a lack of practicality in their work. 'Doing' applies to music, art and history every bit as much as technology, but the vocational link, so important to young people out of love with abstraction, is much more tenuous for them in the former subjects.

'There are no jobs for these kids'. Those of us who were teaching in the 1960s will remember the effortless movement from end of school to start of work. This process is now supplanted by a movement towards a training scheme, or further education for some, but still there is a dearth of sympathetic workplaces thereafter. 'Sympathy' implies fellow-feeling, appropriate tasks, honesty in personal dealings, firm rules and smiling friendship. Those who try to find work for less qualified and less willing eighteen year-olds report an increasing shortage of real vacancies and resistance from putative employers. So, the dole waits, inexorably, for most young people of the kind I have worked with for twenty-five years.

So much has been written about the re-invigoration of the curriculum, (ranging from 'alternative' debates to the appropriateness of the National Curriculum), that it would be wasteful to discuss it here. Let us just say that the more interesting and applicable and fun it is, the more likely it will be that disinclined teenagers will turn to it. But then what? Often they will move from a stimulating educational environment into a, let us say, slightly different training environment (though I know of training agents who will say quite the opposite). Although young people may choose the kind of training they receive, the lower their ability, the more narrow their real chance becomes. Since there is no statutory requirement for training schemes of a particular kind to be available, provision is very patchy (even though there is a requirement that a training place of some description is there for all who require one), local authorities tended to provide more specialized schemes, often with subsidy, but pressure on costs has caused many of these facilities to close. The private and voluntary sectors mostly fill the gap, but market forces stop this being an even process.

Schools have never been encouraged to run their own schemes, nor have they seen it as part of their remit. Heads might, with justification, say that they have enough to worry about without taking on responsibilities which have been in further education, or outside education altogether. However, if they do so, they miss the opportunity to make a contribution to a seamless process.

When education and training are run by the same person in the same place, there is no need for them to be seen as alternatives. Training becomes vocational education, and education becomes a preparation for adult life. In a youth village, the distinction is false, and young people see the process as a sliding scale rather than as a flight of steps. Even the pay differential between students and trainees can be partly removed, since Enterprise education can be organized to create a service, a profit or both. Children of school age respond very well to 'being enterprising', and if this leads to money-making, so be it. Success in this area helps to lessen the difference between those receiving training allowances ('YTS wages') and education students who are not.

A bad Youth Training Scheme is held in even lower esteem by young people than bad education. 'Slave labour' is the cliché they often employ. However, a good placement sees many of them flourish as never before. The requirements of 'goodness' seems to be purposeful, interesting activity, a development of identity by becoming productive or useful, variety in skills being taught, an alternative set of surroundings and social expectations and, amongst others, appropriate qualifications and the real chance of a job afterwards. In addition, it must be undertaken in a good atmosphere, with adult interactions between trainer and trainee.

The presence of good training alongside good special education adds a dynamic to the whole enterprise. The continuity of people and place is ideal, particularly if the type of person a student trainee can be is allowed to change as s/he becomes older or more skilled, or, let us hope, both. *How* you are in such circumstances is just as important as *what* you are.

Special needs educators, therefore, are ideally suited for the task of creating a unity rather than a polarity between education and training. The young people with whom they work start to thrive in predictable, secure yet challenging environments, so if the challenge can be provided as a modern extra ingredient to the traditional mixture of predictability and security, success should follow.

But what is success in this context? Just as education can be valuable, even if there is no obvious vocational or further educational pay off at the end, so training can be enjoyable for its own sake. Indeed, it has to be so for many trainees, particularly if the scheme is of indifferent quality or the area in which it is sited is particularly bereft of job vacancies. Getting a job against the odds is one of life's triumphs for people at the bottom of the social heap. It can bring liberation from penury, freedom to go out and spend, but best of all, it can bring the capacity to be good at something. The likelihood of being 'good' is far greater if the facility is nearby, is linked to what you did before and if you already know the people who run the facility. Equally, the costs are less if the facility is on a site shared with education. The relationship between education, training and special employment should be symbiotic, with the possibility to move slowly or quickly along a continuum of provision rather than a series of disconnected processes. The centralization of administration and decision-making means that choices can be reversed, slowed down or speeded up. In addition, flexibility is achieved in staff deployment, work experience and career development.

The employment element of the community should be based on what can be called 'sympathetic' skills. These should involve natural materials, such as wood, clay or leather, work with which can accommodate a wide variety of skill levels. This is demonstrated in the quality of work produced for almost a century in special school settings. The recent unearthing of an article from 1908 showed what we would now call 'people with special needs' cobbling boots, making chairs and pottery. The context appears medieval, but is it really so inappropriate? The training was appropriate to the time, it increased the chances of subsequent employment, and what is more, there is a likelihood that the work was enjoyable. What was wrong, however, was that there was no choice for the participants. Society was rigidly delineated and people fitted the activity rather than vice versa.

A modern day lesson to be learned is that vocational enterprises, work places targeted on provision for particular people are more needed, not less, and that the integrationist stampede of the early 1980s did a disservice to the chances of certain groups ever finding and keeping enjoyable and productive work. Too often the move into integrated settings devalued the particular life-long needs of groups such as the deaf or older children with emotional and behavioural difficulties. When the needs of a group become diffuse within a larger group, self-image may rise, but the expectation that appropriate provision will appear is idealistic. In Germany businesses will readily pay fines rather than take on their quota of employees with special needs. It is time to say that there is no shame in targeting a place of employment for a given group of people: to achieve progress now we must change focus from the general philosophy of equal opportunities to the particular needs of given groups. This is not to say that all provision should be independent or introspective; it should be based in the community and directed towards it, facing out into society, drawing on the substantial charity organization in this country. It should find subsidy but aim for self-sufficiency. It would require some skilled craftsmen and women to maintain quality throughout, and to generate sufficient output to offset the labour costs of less skilled employees. There should be a range of products and tasks, so that young people of all sorts might be accommodated.

The funding for employment facilities has to come from a wide variety of sources. If you are in an inner city area, the task will be easier to fund, but harder to run: in a rural area it will be easier to run, but harder to fund. The Department of Employment and Industry are always looking for innovative projects which will lift disadvantaged people out of unemployment. However, you must be aware that they are only likely to support projects which show an intention to become self-financing. Charitable trusts and philanthropists can be relied on for early support, providing that you can clearly say what you are proposing, and you can demonstrate how it will help the prospective clients. You are more likely to get grants for equipment than salaries from charities, but Government departments are interested in paying salaries if by doing so they see the measurable expansion of real employment opportunities. Local authorities will help, particularly if they have Economic Development sections, but a great deal of what they do depends on National Government finance, so application to them can be a movable feast. You are more likely to be successful if you can form a limited company and become a registered charity.

When drawing up a business plan for the employment facility, it will become obvious that there is a large interaction between a workshop and the housing needs of young people. Their ability to house themselves, or to get along well with other members of their families under a communal roof, depends very heavily upon the level of their income. Equally, their capacity to successfully fulfil the demands of a job depends heavily upon the circumstances under which they are housed. By the time many prospective clients reach their late teenage years, parents are either not together, or one has died, or are approaching later middle age. Often, one or a combination of these factors adds stress to the housing scene. Relationships form and clients wish to marry or cohabit. Sometimes there is a baby, either on the way or arrived, and several worlds change forever. Simply offering one element of the four-part package of need at such a time, without reference to the others, ensures that life remains compartmentalized and alienation ensues.

The growth of Housing Associations has coincided with the decline in Council Housing Departments. The Housing Corporation now calls the tune with finance for new developments. The change has meant greater flexibility for the charitable entrepreneur or voluntary organization. There is less political by-play, and providing you can convince a Housing Association, of which there will be several in any area, you can get on their priority list for funding application from the Corporation. If you are really ambitious, you can form your own Association!

Most larger Associations have Special Needs Project Officers who will help you to design a scheme. The assumption, of course, is that you have a site, but most schools do have space, even if the land belongs to the local authority. This presupposes political support for the use of the land for purposes other than open space or playing fields: the same applies for the building of an employment facility. Approached sensitively, it is possible to lease council land for the development of activities linked to special needs education. At first the obstacles seem insurmountable, but there are precedents which can be quoted, and with skill and the support of key people success is possible. It is essential not to take 'no' for an answer.

The most useful type of housing development is that which serves two purposes: firstly as a permanent home for people with a considerable difficulty who may always be sole occupants, and secondly as a first step on the housing ladder for people who will raise a family. Both groups need work, of course, but for the former it is more important that the work is nearby. When the management of both facilities is unified, continuity can be assured, and an entire 'deal' can be done with such as Social Services or the voluntary sector for the realization of potential in underfunctioning and under privileged young adults.

Recent years have seen encouragement given to entrepreneurs, particularly in run-down urban areas. This has not been matched by a keen response from educationalists, who, by and large, have felt beleaguered and unloved, and in whom there is no history of straying into other areas of social need. A joining together of different backgrounds is required, but with educationalists and trainers at the centre, thus maintaining a client-centredness as the core of the four-part enterprise.

So there we have it. A place, where the majority of clients come for education. Some of these, along with late entrants, move on to various kinds of training provided by the same host organization. On site, but separated somewhat, is an employment facility which creates work experience for many, training and short-term employment for several and permanent employment for a few. Nearby is a housing development which offers short-term accommodation for some, and emergency or permanent housing for a few.

Why should this be? It exists to create a very real set of services and opportunities for disadvantaged people, but it is also designed as a statement about the true significance of people at the bottom of the heap. The process bypasses the traditional notions of educational integration, which was based on the ideas of a generation past and heads straight for the community, in order to empower young people to learn, train, work and be housed decently, and as they would wish. It is also a more elegant use of public money than pouring it down the dole drain. The author has, at the time of writing, developed three of these facilities in one setting, and hopes to add the fourth as soon as funds become available. It has become an exhausting life's work.

CHAPTER 6

Rethinking the Role of the Special Needs Co-ordinator : Devolving the Remedial Department

Jean Luscombe

The story of the school

For the past twenty years I have been responsible for work with children with special educational needs at Cirencester Deer Park School. This chapter tells the story of how we have moved from special classes and remedial teaching, through the notion of in-class support and of a Learning Skills Centre, to the point where we now believe that provision for all and support for the learning of all is so embedded in the structure of the school that it is no longer necessary to have a single person 'responsible' for special needs (see Figure 1 for an historical summary). It may be that our story will indicate the way that provision for individual differences will develop in many more schools as we approach the year 2000.

Figure 1

Historical Summary of Developments at Deer Park School

1972   Formation of Remedial Department
        Work on physical environment
        Exploration of teaching styles and children's potential

1978   Warnock Report : leading to briefings for staff; issue of
        integration raised
        Explorations of mixed-ability teaching

1985   Establishment of Learning Skills as a service department
        Continuing development of teaching styles across cur-
        riculum

1986   Opening of Learning Skills Centre

1988   County LAPS scheme introduced with Humanities
        Department

1989   Formulation of Learning Skills policy document

1991   Introduction of curriculum counselling
        Devolution of Learning Skills Centre to faculty learning
        centres

1992   Retirement of Head of Learning Skills

Cirencester Deer Park School has an interesting history established
on a foundation of integration and flexibility in its search to provide
educational excellence for the community it serves. The school at
present boasts to be a 'liberal institution with rigorous academic
standards' which:

- convinces pupils that they can achieve more than they first
  thought
- pupils take pride in and enjoy coming to
- aims for seamless primary/secondary/tertiary transition
- is a lead school in its delivery of the National Curriculum
- has a commitment to quality in all aspects of its work

The school has always believed in its potential and has striven
to meet change and search for excellence in a positive equitable
manner through natural development.

The original comprehensive, an eight-form, mixed-entry school
formed in 1966, was an amalgamation of a 500 year old mixed
three-form entry grammar school and two three-form entry, mixed,
single-sex modern schools. Such devastating reorganization needed
gentle and careful planning, a criterion that has always been high
on the agenda of the school's continuing development.

The curriculum was organized into horizontal divisions of Junior, Intermediate and VI Form Studies, which, twenty six years later, is comparable to Key Stages 3 and 4 and the Tertiary College! There were also vertical divisions of Houses, the basis of the school's present strong emphasis on the pastoral system. The tutor groups were mixed ability and at this time students were taught in such groups for practical subjects and Religious Education. The rest of the curriculum was taught in three graded ability bands. At the same time it was said that 'staff had shown a willingness to teach children of differing abilities, that is, certain members of the former modern school staff teach to 'O' and 'A' level, others of the former grammar school teach some of the lower ability sets.' Here, one might say, were the beginnings of equality of curriculum delivery.

By 1972 it was believed that some students were 'remedial' and needed specialist teaching and a different curriculum to meet their needs and so as not to hamper the development of the 'average' and 'high flying' pupil. A group of approximately sixteen formed the remedial class of each year, being taught by the same five teachers for all subjects. It was a sad day when such segregation was thought necessary for the benefit of both staff and pupils. What a good thing that no longer were pupils to feel their inadequacies through not mixing with their peer group; it was clearly far better to be isolated and have these inadequacies highlighted by being considered bottom of the pile! Staff were relieved the frustration of teaching high and low bands in quick succession – the lower groups so difficult to 'get down to' – rather than be given the experience of learning differing teaching strategies and beginning to understand the individual needs of a full range of ability.

A lot of teacher learning was necessary and a lot of questions needed answering. Why were these pupils not successful? Were they worth spending time and energy on? Could they ever mix and successfully be accepted by their peer group? Could they ever be the responsibility of all staff and departments? Could they benefit from equality of opportunity? Could they ever be fully integrated into the main curriculum? Could the school ever reach the stage where it was stated that the key feature of the Head of Department's role is to ensure that all pupils receive the same high quality education within their curriculum area?

First steps : 1972–77

Although in those early days we could not control the way the school was organized or the pupils were grouped, there were things in our own work that we *could* control. A priority easily achieved with instant results was improvement to décor. Creating a pleasant working environment began to inculcate a feeling of well-being, ownership and worth. Any rooms the Remedial Department were allocated were first painted. This included the sanding and varnishing of desk tops. Not surprisingly, the pupils responded and accommodation continued to look good.

We could also control our own teaching. We had our own freedom to teach as we wished, because nobody really bothered what we did! This is where I learned how to teach these children and just how very much I could expect of them. Learning and sharing experiences with these pupils was most invigorating and rewarding. We discovered that when alternatives to writing were found it was astounding and exciting to understand their depth of feeling and grasp of subject matter. And role play, tape recordings, model making, puppetry, videos, plays performed to outside venues, all gave sufficient methods of communication and confidence to tackle writing and spelling issues, which always seemed to be the main weakness. The pupils' potential, it seemed, was determined at least as much by how they were taught as by their own innate difficulties.

The move to Learning Skills : 1978–89

As we were developing our work in isolation, there were moves within the wider school and, indeed, nationally, that were to bear fruit for us. Within the school, there was a gradual move towards mixed ability teaching. This move was by no means dramatic. As the then head, David Saunders wrote in 1986:

> These moves have taken place slowly and have always waited until suitable new courses have been introduced. Staff, too, have had to be prepared to make the move and, on occasion, it has been necessary to await staff changes before progress could be made.

At the same time, the Warnock Report (DES 1978) brought our case to the fore. It was an opportune moment for more serious papers to be written regarding our development. Staff were briefed on both the Report and its implications for Deer Park School. It also seemed opportune to suggest ideas for the integration of all pupils into the mixed ability group.

The next step was to remove the label 'Remedial'. What were we trying to remedy? The name calling? The acceptance of being no good? The worthlessness of not being examination pupils? We were certainly all learning; we were certainly all improving our skills, both staff and pupils alike. So the new label became LEARNING SKILLS. And once again the accommodation became a key feature in breaking barriers. We moved from our humble, condemned terrapins to, eventually, a Learning Skills Centre, well-appointed, carpeted, curtained, highly-resourced and large enough to cater for up to fifty pupils engrossed in multi-activities.

Alongside the new name and new venue grew a consultancy model in which both pupils and staff could come for advice and share practical skills. The room was open from 8-30 a.m. to 5-00 p.m. daily, and an increasingly wide range of pupils used it – not simply those who were labelled 'special needs'. Indeed, this was part of a deliberate move away from the idea of 'the SEN child' as someone who was suffering from some long-term and global difficulty which affected her/his attainments right across the curriculum. We prefer instead an idea of special needs as needs which arise in particular children at particular times within particular curriculum contexts. Special needs for us, therefore, is not an indication of innate disabilities in the child, but of the need for the teachers to modify their teaching.

Accordingly, we saw ourselves as a service department not just for pupils, but also for staff. Colleagues were able to come to the Learning Skills Centre to team teach with us. They were able to experiment with teaching styles – styles that might have seemed risky in the isolation of their own classrooms – within a context of support from resources, from staffing, and from professional trust. Indeed, in the same spirit, we opened up the Learning Skills Centre to staff from other schools in the area, keeping 'open house' for materials to be borrowed and ideas to be shared.

We learned that, if two or more departments were to work together, commitment and support for clear objectives were necessary so that we could review and evaluate departmental methods for using the facilities provided by Learning Skills. At all times, Learning Skills acted as a support service and only staff and departments who wanted to become involved took part. This shift of emphasis was helped enormously by our involvement in the Less Able Pupils Support (LAPS – Gloucestershire's version of the LAPP) project. This gave us £3000 and the services of a support teacher for a year, enabling us to work with the Humanities Department on a resource-based curriculum for the third year pupils. Thus we broke out of the special needs 'ghetto' of working only with the English Department and only with younger pupils, but we were able to do so by offering colleagues positive advantages and bonuses for working with us.

It soon seemed necessary to clarify our role both for our own sakes and in order to be explicit about our expectations of colleagues working with us. To help us do this – and as part of our 'open house' approach – we invited Maria Landy, then the local authority special needs adviser, to work with us on developing the following policy statement:

Learning Skills policy

Philosophy

The Learning Skills Team is an integral part of the 'Whole School' system, 11–19. It endeavours to supply the necessary back-up for both pupils and staff to enable all children to take advantage of the equal opportunities policy that the Deer Park School advocates, with special emphasis on helping those with special needs.

Aims

i)   to provide for the individual needs of all pupils
ii)   to have a flexible framework within which it can adapt and implement new ideas in response to special needs
iii) to provide help in identifying pupils with special needs and to see that appropriate records are kept
iv)   to further the process of integration of special needs children into the normal classroom situation and to co-ordinate the provision for these children
v)   to provide a relevant, realistic, balanced and broad curriculum but with a differentiated response to individual needs
vi)   to promote optimum use of existing resources to these ends (both Learning Skills and departmental) – staff, accommodation, equipment and materials

vii) to provide appropriate in-service training and support for all staff

viii) to upgrade constantly and review annually Learning Skills policy, practices and materials

ix) to be aware of and to respond to local and national services and initiatives

Recent developments: the 1990s

Recent years have seen a continuation – even an acceleration – of the process of devolution. The experimentation with teaching styles which has long been a characteristic of our work and which we tried to encourage through the Learning Skills Centre, has increasingly become a characteristic of work throughout the school. Mixed ability teaching has suggested that most children in 'Warnock's eighteen per cent' probably had a mismatch between their abilities, attitudes, hopes and the diet provided for them by the school. It is our belief that working in mixed ability groups brings about an understanding of abilities, needs and character that cannot begin to be understood in narrow singular environments.

This has implications for teaching methods. We believe that a variety of lesson presentations will reach and satisfy a greater proportion of pupils, hopefully inculcating a desire and will to learn. Across the school, therefore, we use a full range of teaching strategies – group work, paired work, videos, drama, role play, linked cross-curricular topics and, increasingly, flexible learning approaches.

These are supported in a variety of ways. The single Learning Skills Centre has been replaced by a range of learning centres performing similar functions. These include a library, jointly staffed by a librarian and a teacher-in-charge; an ICL computer room, staffed by a technician; a mathematics computer room with staffing provided by the mathematics department; and English resource/teaching room, staffed by the English department on a lunch-time rota; a humanities resource/teaching room which I help to staff; a technology computer room with teacher supervision; and science laboratories which are also open to pupils in off-timetable times. In all of these venues teaching is available on a one-to-one basis and a multitude of resources activate pupils' own learning. If these rooms are to be available as genuine pupil resource areas then it is necessary that they are accessible for more than simply lesson times. Thus help is often available before school, at breaktime, at lunchtime and at 'curriculum extension' time from 3.30–4.30 p.m.

This learning centre approach is part of a general emphasis within the school on the pupil's own responsibility for learning. More often than not, this approach is successful, probably because there is a back-up system to support it. A 'curriculum counselling' time is in operation whereby pupils who, for whatever reason, are not reaching their full potential receive guidance, firstly to analyse the problem and secondly to put possible strategies for solving the problem into operation. This counselling is offered by members of the 'pastoral team'. As a shared experience between pupil and head of year, it is advantageous not only for the pastoral system but also for the curriculum module where the problem is occurring. It could be said that *the pastoral team is the quality controller representing the pupil in ensuring a differentiated curriculum delivery.*

A third form of support for our mixed ability teaching strategies comes from a team of faculty representatives who work with me and within their own areas on special needs issues. If, as I said earlier, we are moving to a view of special needs as arising in particular curriculum contexts, then responsibility for meeting special needs has to rest with curriculum areas. Accordingly, there are additional resources available to faculties for making special needs provision. However, to gain access to these resources, faculties have to make a case, identifying the needs they see in their own area and showing how the resources would be used to meet those needs. There is, therefore, an incentive for faculties to keep special needs high on their agendas and to continue the process of development. (There is also – and this is becoming increasingly important – a means of ensuring that resources intended for special needs are actually spent on special needs.)

These, however, are simply the most obvious strategies we have at our disposal. When special needs provision is the responsibility of a Special Needs Department, it is relatively easy to describe and analyse it; it is also relatively easy to see who is responsible for it and to enforce some form of accountability. However, when that responsibility is devolved throughout the school, as it is beginning to be at Deer Park, it is much more difficult to say exactly what the special needs provision *is* and who precisely does what to make it work. The danger is that, when responsibility is devolved, it should be everybody's but ends up being nobody's. We have tried, therefore, to use some of the ideas of systems thinking (see Frederickson in Chapter One) to map out our provision for individual differences (Figures 2 and 3).

It is possible to think of the school as a whole as a *system for enabling all pupils to learn effectively*. It is helpful to think of it as comprising a number of sub-systems, each with their own components. Hence, the bulk of the work of teachers-in-faculties forms a *curriculum-delivery system*, a set of strategies for trying to ensure that all pupils receive appropriate and effective learning experiences. Those experiences, and the work of teachers in structuring those experiences, are supplemented by a *curriculum support system* which enhances what the teacher in the classroom can offer. Their effectiveness is monitored by a *pupil-in-curriculum monitoring system* which is concerned not simply with assessing pupil 'progress' but with looking at the interactions between the pupil and the curriculum on offer. Where those interactions – and hence the learning that should result from them – break down, we can call upon a *break-down system* which feeds back into the curriculum support system to put things right. And the whole is monitored by a *school monitoring and control system* which allows us to determine how we are doing, to take corrective action, and to continue the process of development.

These 'systems' do not, of course, correspond to the visible features of the school's organization. They are a way of thinking about a whole range of activities, carried out by a whole range of teachers quite separately from each other, as coherent wholes. They also allow us to list those activities (Figure 3), and this gives us some means of checking the overall balance and effectiveness of our work. Whatever else this shows, it makes it clear that Learning Skills no longer exists as one person, one room, selected pupils, simply because it has been devolved and is now an accepted and working feature in all faculties.

A whole school learning has occurred. Questions have been answered, more have taken their place – and this is to be expected if the school is a lively, demanding and challenging environment. We are now, once again, therefore, on the verge of a major development. If special needs provision has been devolved successfully to the school as a whole, then I, as Head of Special Needs, am no longer necessary. Indeed, if I stay in that role, then 'special needs' will revert to being me carrying things through. After twenty years in post, therefore, I shall be

Figure 2 A model of provision for individual differences at Deer Park School

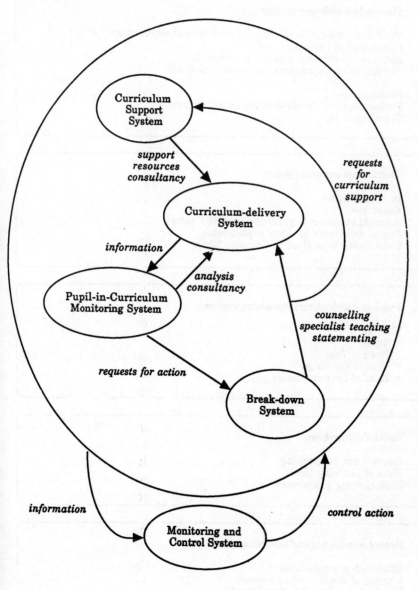

Figure 3   Current practice related to the sub-systems

Curriculum-delivery system

Tight and predictable schemes of work with common tasks
Differentiated teaching
Skills re-inforcement within the curriculum
Flexibility within subjects [e.g. modularization]

Facilitated by ...
Decision-making devolved to departmental level
Team approach

Curriculum support system

In class support
Resources
External resources [e.g. Library and IT Centre]
Pupils' experience in other departments
Consultancy from Head of Learning Skills

Pupil-in-curriculum monitoring system

Work of
• Tutor
• Head of Year
• Head of Key Stage
• Head of Learning Skills

Break-down system

Curriculum counselling
Head of Learning Skills
Statementing procedures

School monitoring and control system

Observation programme
Logging of use of in-class support
Heads of year log contact with pupils

taking early retirement at the end of the current academic year.

Implications

Does our experience at Deer Park School have any implications for other schools – indeed for the future direction of special needs provision in mainstream schools? Certainly, one implication is that change cannot be brought about overnight. I had the dream of what was possible nearly twenty years ago, working in the old Remedial Department, when I realized just what the children were capable of. But I have had to wait to see that dream unfold.

There is also an implication to do with the sort of school in which such developments are possible. Deer Park has a common mission brought about by good team spirit, where there are shared values, clear goals and instructional leadership. The school emphasis is on high quality teaching and learning which continually aim for excellence. *All* students are expected to fulfil their potential and responsibilities to and for the school environment. And the focus is on a model that is not static. Continual whole-school monitoring, assessment and feedback means innovatory practice is encouraged and ongoing. In fact, a logical next step for us would be to carry out some form of detailed audit of the needs that exist in our school. We suspect that most schools have no very clear picture of what their pupils need, simply because no one has ever looked!

Part of the common mission is that the school sees itself as open to anyone in the area who wishes to come to us, and is willing to adapt to their special needs rather than expecting them to adapt to us. As the present Development Plan states:

> We offer an entitlement curriculum for all. This aims to leave all post 16 academic and career options open. We teach in both mixed ability and setted classes as appropriate to the needs of the subject. We have put a particular emphasis on Learning Skills support both outside and inside the classroom. We aim to be a lead school in our response to the National Curriculum and have sought actively to enhance parental understanding of it.

In all of this, the Head is the key. He has been – and has to be – a true believer in the developments that are taking place, if for no other reason than that a 'devolved' form of provision involves the whole school and has to be managed from the centre of the school – not from its periphery.

All of this is to do with the culture of the school and the process of change. In terms of the form of provision, our experience suggests that, *if there is a working alternative system* in operation, there will no longer need to be one person responsible for special needs. The responsibility belongs to the whole school and as such the special needs pupil becomes the norm and accepted as part of the annual intake to a comprehensive school. Individual needs can then be recognized and understood. A well-planned, forward-thinking and caring school community will do all in its power to meet these needs as part of its commitment in providing an education that fulfils the aims of the National Curriculum.

As Ron Dawson says,

> Surely, education is the celebration of happiness, the joy of childhood, the joy of learning, caring for others, meeting individual needs and respecting the individual. (Private lecture)

This is a time of quite incredible changes in education – its beliefs, structure and practice. Success will depend on how the school answers the call for a broad, balanced, relevant and differentiated curriculum, remembering, of course, that it is an entitlement curriculum for *ALL* children.

Reference

Department of Education and Science (1978) *Special Educational Needs (The Warnock Report)*. London: HMSO.

CHAPTER 7

Rethinking the Role of the Special Needs Co-ordinator: the Quality Assurer

Janet Simpson

I did not set out to be a special needs teacher. I was inspired by the energy and commitment of a Special Needs Department in a school where I was on teaching practice. Mostly, I am grateful to them for their inspiration; occasionally I curse them! During the fifteen years I have worked in special needs I have operated in a variety of ways: special classes, withdrawal groups, individual appointments, in-class support. All in mainstream secondary schools and all deemed necessary because the mainstream curriculum was devised for 'average' pupils, with roughly the same content, level and pace for all.

Until recently I did not question this. Increasingly though I began to feel that this concentration on individual pupils and their needs without considering the context of the whole curriculum was somewhat blinkered. Yet developments in the field of special needs continued to be very much based around individual needs. There was a notion that we could 'top up' the skills of the pupils we were responsible for so that they could 'cope' with the mainstream curriculum. I realized that some fundamental assumptions about the mainstream curriculum needed challenging. In the same way I did not originally set out to be a special needs teacher, so I did not set out to be a quality assurer; it grew naturally out of whole-school developments and my personal commitment to individual learning.

I was appointed as the Head of Special Needs at William Howard School in 1985. It is an 11–18, six-form entry comprehensive school with a large rural catchment area. A system of small-group withdrawal was operating, the underlying assumption being that we could 'change' the children and somehow ensure that they could have access to an inappropriate mainstream curriculum. Ironically, the fact that they were not part of the mainstream curriculum inevitably meant that it would not become appropriate or accessible. However, it is only in retrospect that this approach seems so misguided. The message from the experience of withdrawing pupils was clearly that pupils should remain in the mainstream and the 'support' would follow them there. Thus the intended change was extended to include child and teacher. This is a costly way of providing support for individual pupils and can only be effective where there is full consultation and real partnership.

In 1988 I was appointed as a senior teacher with a whole-school responsibility for differentation. Initially, consideration was given to another group of pupils with special educational needs: the most able. A wide range of ability within teaching groups makes it difficult to encourage the full potential of the pupils at either end of the ability range. We knew that recent developments had gone some way to ensuring that the least able could be supported to achieve their full potential. However, evidence that no such mechanisms existed for the most able.

I was conscious that my rise to the level of the senior management team was viewed with some scepticism and so wanted to make an impact and provide a 'trigger' for the kind of action which would be effective and make a difference. There appear to be four ways of delivering an appropriate curriculum for the most able:

1. an effective differentation programme in classrooms
2. ability grouping
3. enrichment programmes
4. acceleration.

Although we were moving in the direction of increasing effective differentiation, there were still significant problem areas. Ability grouping is employed with the older pupils and for many well-rehearsed reasons we were not keen to rely on this entirely with younger pupils. The enrichment programme involves taking pupils off timetable for a whole week and affording them the opportunity of working with subject specialist teachers and outside experts on specific projects. Some examples have been working with

• archaeologists at Birdoswald Roman Fort,

- North-West Water on water analysis,
- a retired classics teacher for an intensive week of Latin,
- a local firm of architects on housing design,
- the editor of a local newspaper.

Analysis of how pupils respond to these experiences and the levels of achievement they attain suggest the type and level of curricular opportunities which should be available in the classroom. We are currently developing processes which will enable us to negotiate and plan individual curricula with pupils.

The introduction of the National Curriculum also provided us with an opportunity further to raise awareness about effective individual learning. Content and skills are now determined for us and developments have concentrated on appropriate teaching and learning styles. Analysis of what actually happens in classrooms has given us evidence that a range of teaching and learning styles is necessary if pupils are to achieve their full potential. For example, radical restructuring of pupil grouping systems by attainment rather than age was rejected in favour of more flexible systems. We are looking to group pupils according to ability and/or interest for *specific* purposes and for *specific* times. Clearly there are implications for the timetable and we now build in significant amounts of block timetabling and look carefully at teacher teams to enable these things to happen.

Developing a quality assurance framework

Analysis of what happens in classrooms has become the central feature of our quality assurance process. It was not the starting point initially. Each year a School Development Plan has been established with consultation and involvement at all levels: governors, senior management team, middle management and staff. In 1989, in an annual review, we asked the basic question: 'How do we know how well we are doing?' This led us to initiate some work on what we considered to be quality in a whole range of activities, and how we could ensure that it was happening. It was, perhaps inadvisedly, called Quality Control. 'Control' is an emotive word and the introduction of other jargon such as 'mission statement', 'targets', 'performance indicators' and 'audits' provoked a great deal of concern. The success of all these developments required a culture shift. I hope that colleagues who initially felt vulnerable and threatened by both the language and associated processes now view them in a more positive and confident way. Progress suggests that this is so.

Previously we had attempted to bring about curricular change through the development of whole school policies. These were formulated through consultation with staff and departments but unfortunately resulted in little significant change. We needed a different approach to bring about sustained and effective curriculum and organizational development. Realizing that failure to meet the individual needs of pupils successfully was rooted in our curriculum provision led me to analyse what *was* currently available. We needed a process which could measure the effectiveness and efficiency of the current curriculum. This would challenge assumptions which are constantly rebuilt into curriculum developments. Colleagues could examine what they were doing and use this as a starting point for rethinking and development.

The framework for the development of quality assurance was the School Development Plan and the target areas identified. Each one consisted of a series of audit questions, performance indicators and instruments/documents. The method of asking a series of questions, and so developing sets of performance indicators which would give information showing whether our intentions had been met, gave a more structured way forward. This was in contrast to previous descriptive accounts of our intentions. A whole-school approach to planning and management could be facilitated by a phased development.

Deciding priorites:

- what are our strengths and weaknesses?
- what do we need to ignore? consolidate? develop?
- who will do what? by when?

Evaluation-led planning:

- what do we want to happen?
- how will we know when it is happening?

Analysis of current situation:

- collection of evidence using interview/questionnaires/diaries/classroom observation.

Implementation:

- where are the priority areas?
- which areas show readiness for development?

The key to this approach is in the question 'How will we know when it is happening?' To answer this question, performance indicators − sets of criteria − would be vital and would serve several purposes. Previous attempts at coherence and consistency had resulted in whole school policies. Criteria communicate an ideal but in a more specific and tangible way than a policy. Analysis is focused on actual classroom practice, particularly learning outcomes. The planning process must begin from the premise that pupils are individuals and the educational process must take this into account. School development plans can only become more consistent and lead to achievement of objectives if there is a facilitating process. A criteria-based observation programme was identified as that process.

Collecting evidence

As we attempted to answer our audit questions and devise performance indicators we found that there was an increasing amount of detail. The performance indicators could be written plans, policies, agreements or lists of criteria which related to classroom practice. Some evidence we needed could only be found by having an observer in the classroom to record classroom practice. This, clearly, was viewed as being very threatening. To overcome this we knew that the whole process had to be 'shared' and 'owned' by those involved. Much discussion and negotiation took place and the atmosphere in which this happened needed to be positive and supportive. In the future I hope that it will become more acceptable for there to be two teachers in a classroom, with one collating evidence which can be used constructively to benefit pupils.

The observation programme has been carried out within departments since January 1991. Those departments which have been involved include: Languages, Science, Technology, Humanities, Mathematics, Drama and Physical Education. External funding from the Training Agency released me from my teaching commitments in the period January − June 1991. The following programme was followed with each department:

1. · meeting with the Head of Department to discuss process

2. meetings with the whole department to discuss process and to negotiate criteria to be used and methods of collecting evidence
3. a programme of observation with detailed recording of evidence
4. a series of statements was collated from the evidence
5. debriefing meetings with department and individuals
6. targets and future action agreed and documented in the departmental development plan.

We have explored ways other than classroom observation for the collection of evidence. For example, we briefed some groups of pupils to keep diaries. We asked them to record their experience during a particular period in a specific curriculum area. Sometimes we gave them specific questions to address, such as 'how many worksheets did you use this week?'; 'how many times did you have to ask the teacher to explain something on the worksheet to you?' Pupils record as they go through the set period of time and we examine the evidence afterwards.

These are some extracts from some pupil diaries kept during a Year 9 Poetry Enrichment Week:

Pupil 1: Today I learned about a monologue. I learned this through the teacher. I worked hard all lesson and I got on with the people in my group. I got on well with the teacher and she helped by explaining things clearly and being helpful. We watched a video and did a worksheet. I think that the worksheet was quite good because it explained the meaning of something clearly in the form of a story. I felt I was quite successful. I completed the work although I had to bring it home to finish. I think we could have done with more time. I did not need a lot of help with the work. I enjoyed the lesson and I liked the teacher. I especially enjoyed the video.

Pupil 2: This lesson was 'weird' and the poem *The Albatross Ramble* extremely so. I did not enjoy this lesson at all, partly because it was difficult to understand and partly because I did not like the group I was in. Also the lesson was very rushed and I got a little bit lost at the end of the lesson as to what I was meant to be doing.

Pupil 3: In today's lesson we started to learn about the Old English poem *Beowulf*. We read the Old English version and then the translation. I thought I worked hard all lesson. I got on with all the people in my group. The teacher was very helpful.

He helped us to understand the Old English words in the poem and he made the poem sound interesting. We did not do much written work but I felt our group oral work was of a high standard and we finished it. I was pleased with the work I had done. The resources were very interesting.

We also used questionnaires in the initial stages to get a 'snapshot' of staff attitudes to the issues related to teaching and learning styles. Staff were asked to respond in terms of agreement or disagreement to a series of statements, for example:

- pupils are identified by the teacher
- pupils take an active role in seeking information
- time spent on activities follows a plan determined by the teacher
- the outcomes of lessons and activities are usually predetermined
- both pupil and teacher have a say in assessment
- learning is a process directed by the teacher
- time is provided in class for reflection and forward planning by pupils.

Developing performance indicators

When we first started looking to more flexible approaches to teaching and learning – in ways more likely to ensure effective individual learning – we made it clear what characteristics would indicate that this was happening.

Flexible learning is where pupils:

- work at their own pace
- work at their own level
- are encouraged to develop their own ideas
- are involved with teachers in negotiating individual targets
- work individually or in small groups
- use a wide range of stimulating resources.

A number of departments in school had been trialling flexible learning strategies and in negotiation with them the following list of criteria was developed. We asked how we would know whether the above things were happening if we were to observe in the classroom. We needed indicators which would let us know that these things were enabling effective individual learning:

- a variety of resources is available for both in-class and out-of-class work
- different pupils work on different tasks selected in part by the pupils. A variety of tasks is available to fit individual requirements.
- learning activities are varied and flexible and pupils are participating fully
- the teacher communicates and negotiates with individuals or small groups rather than with the whole group
- the teacher's talk and questioning varies in type and difficulty for different pupils to ensure understanding.
- the teacher adopts the role of enabler and facilitator. Pupils contribute to the direction of the lesson and can initiate and negotiate activities
- the time allowed for pupils to complete a given task must vary according to individual differences. Support and extension activities must be planned for
- evaluation should occur in relation to individual pupils and identify and record progress and achievement.

In other departments, Technology for example, the emphasis was rather different and they used a range of criteria which reflected the planning, designing, making and evaluating cycle of teaching and learning:

- pupils know what they should be doing and can tell someone about their current task
- pupils understand why they are carrying out the task and how it fits in to the learning experience
- pupils have been given opportunities to be involved in the planning of tasks where appropriate
- pupils are given opportunities to discuss work in progress with teachers and each other
- where appropriate, pupils are given opportunities to choose the task, what they need and the way in which they work
- pupils spend a high proportion of time on the task
- pupils are fully engaged in the task
- pupils can use a variety of resources
- pupils interact whilst working together in groups
- pupils contribute to group tasks

- pupils are involved in a variety of tasks
- pupils use an appropriate range of skills.

Using such sets of criteria as the basis for the collection of evidence through observation in the classroom is the next stage. Undoubtedly my colleagues felt threatened by this. However, many staff were used to me being in the classroom working alongside them to support the learning of some pupils, and, while the role was clearly different, they soon adjusted. Consideration does need to be given to who does the observation; we involved our head teacher in an evaluation of one of the flexible learning modules in English and the effect that had on behaviour in the classroom was very evident.

Other aspects of classroom observation which must be considered carefully are the nature of recording and the timing and nature of the feedback. I have not set out to be judgemental about anything I have observed. The information which is recorded is factual and observable. Instinctively many of us have a tendency to be critical or judgemental when observing classroom practice. The whole purpose of the observation I have carried out has been that the information recorded be used to establish a dialogue with individual colleagues; *they* draw conclusions, reflect upon them and identify ways to develop and, if appropriate, improve the quality of teaching and learning in the classroom.

This process is also undertaken by whole departments. All the information is collated and a series of statements put together. Here are two examples:

Science Department – statements collated from evidence:
- modules of work are written to the same formula. Activities/information generally start at a low level and gradually move through to activities/information at higher levels
- all pupils start at the beginning of the module and work through the tasks in order
- pupils in mixed ability teaching groups work in single-sex friendship groups for experimental/investigational work
- in the majority of lessons, observed pupils work on the same tasks/series of tasks
- tasks and information are presented to the pupils on worksheets in all lessons observed
- pupils are frequently given step-by-step instructions in order to carry out experimental/investigational tasks

- much of the extension and support work is intuitive on the part of the teacher and not systematically built into the modules of work
- a range of resources is used, although pupils rarely have access to reference or text books
- slower and/or less able pupils take much longer to complete practical work
- differentiation by outcome is most effective when there is specific intervention/targeting on the part of a teacher.

Languages Department – statements collated from evidence:
- the pattern of activities in languages lessons is very similar and tends to be a series of short tasks
- in groups of higher ability, pupils work at a quicker pace and undertake tasks of greater complexity
- tasks are greatly simplified for groups of lower ability pupils and the slower pace allows for appropriate reinforcement
- the listening activities are a crucial feature of languages teaching and learning. 'Active' listening is a difficult activity to monitor and assess
- the participative nature of the activities militates against those pupils who are quiet and introverted and less inclined to involve themselves in whole class activities
- generally all pupils in the teaching groups undertake the same tasks
- the time allowed for pupils to complete tasks is the same for all and frequently means that some pupils finish well within the time and some others are unable to complete tasks
- assessment and evaluation is built into the courses in the form of unit tests and graded tests but less effectively included in lessons
- pupils are not given the same opportunities to demonstrate their language skills.

Conclusions

There have been many common themes which have emerged. Consideration of issues related to resources, teacher-pupil interaction, tasks pupils undertake, evaluation and reflection, effective communication, motivation, educational objectives, outcomes, information processing, and a wide range of accompanying areas has led to departments re-assessing their current curricular provision. Often trials or pilot schemes have been set up and evaluated using the same sets of criteria.

Systematic and rigorous analysis of classroom activity will provide information and evidence to be used when drawing up departmental development plans and the school staff development plan. The quality assurance programme has created a climate where it is now accepted as a potent tool in the planning, implementation and evaluation of curricular developments. The challenging of many assumptions about teaching and learning styles has enabled many staff to reflect constructively about what takes place in the classroom. It has also supported the view that a variety of teaching and learning styles and contexts is necessary to ensure effective learning. Also, individual staff must be able to operate effectively and comfortably in a given situation; they must not feel that they are being advised that a particular style is more acceptable.

The process has been a valuable tool for getting heads of department into the management of teaching and learning in their departments, on a very different level from the operational one which looks at the deployment of staff and resources and the day-to-day running of a department. The analysis of the learning process and pupil outcomes which takes place during the observation programmes will encourage the teaching and learning style issue to be considered alongside that of content in the planning stage. Line management is now falling into place and the evidence collected in the observation programme is enabling us to build annual review and evaluation into departmental development plans and into individual job descriptions.

I believe that the process of quality assurance has important implications in examining curricular provision for all pupils. In particular, for pupils with special educational needs, it identifies difficulties of access to the mainstream curriculum; it attempts to ensure that *all* pupils can learn effectively, including those with special educational needs. It was becoming increasingly clear that the support necessary to ensure access for these pupils was not available or, unfortunately, not affordable. The restructuring of our school curriculum will, I hope, promote the individual learning of those pupils with special educational needs. This restructuring is based around more flexible grouping arrangements, an increase in the range and variety of resources, mechanisms to enable pupils to work at their own pace and level, tutoring based on negotiation and the setting of targets, the setting of educational outcomes and agreement about evidence that they have been achieved. I am optimistic that it will lead to more effective learning for all pupils. It will also, hopefully, lead to a reassessment of the definition of pupils with special educational needs: there should no longer be a group of pupils for whom the mainstream curriculum is inappropriate.

CHAPTER 8

Rethinking the Role of the Special Needs Co-ordinator: the Institutional Developer

Elizabeth Scott

The debate about the changing nature of special educational needs provision in mainstream schools predates Warnock (D.E.S. 1978), and has steadily gathered momentum during the 1980s. In particular, much has been written about the changing role of the special needs co-ordinator, (Bines 1986, Butt 1986, 1991, Dyson 1990, 1991, 1992). The rhetoric surrounding these changes has been to do with principles that most teachers would readily accept – equal opportunity and a fundamental human right of educational entitlement. The real question, however, is the extent to which these principles can be and actually have been translated into daily practice.

There are, I would suggest, a series of barriers to the easy implementation in mainstream schools of changes in our thinking about special needs. These barriers are to do with the culture of those schools, with the nature of the values and beliefs of the individuals who work within them and with the pressures and constraints under which schools and teachers work. They might include:

- the pressures on schools to ensure academic achievement, defined narrowly so as to exclude the achievements and capabilities of children with special needs
- a lack of confidence on the part of mainstream teachers in their ability to deliver quality education to *all* children
- a failure on the part of those involved in the special needs debate sufficiently to involve their mainstream colleagues in the change in thinking
- a sustained period of uncertainty and upheaval in education, resulting in 'innovation fatigue' amongst many teachers and

- a sincere belief on the part of many mainstream teachers in existing practices.

Whether or not these barriers ever amount to a direct intention to block or prevent change on the part of mainstream teachers and schools, they do have implications for the task that has been set for special needs co-ordinators as the pivot for changes in special needs provision and practice. They have to recognize and be prepared for facing these barriers whilst at the same time accepting vastly changed expectations of their role.

Traditionally the role of the special needs co-ordinator focused around an ability to teach basic skills. The training that was available reinforced this notion with practical courses which stressed immediate pupil contact as the major weapon in their armoury. What these co-ordinators now need, however, is training that is embedded in the microculture of the school in which they work. They are not now only being asked to be 'remedial teachers' or specialist skill holders, but curriculum consultants, advisers and co-operative teachers. At the same time, they are being warned that, if they cannot find a way to provide a value-added component to education (Butt 1991), they will become, as Dyson (1990) threatens, a 'dying breed'.

These changes were all beginning to happen when there was a massive cut-back in training budgets. No longer were secondments available, and longer courses gave way to the shorter SENIOS (Special Educational Needs in Ordinary Schools) model. So how should special needs co-ordinators proceed? Clearly, *they had to become involved in planning and managing their own change and development whilst not losing sight of the most important aspect of their very existence, their responsibility as guardians and advocates of the rights of special needs pupils.*

The self-developing special needs co-ordinator

There are two main areas, I believe, that special needs co-ordinators should consider in developing their role:

- ensuring that the needs of children are met in terms of their total curriculum
- facilitating the involvement of *all* colleagues in a generic pattern of special needs provision.

These are significant changes in role requirement. Both the special needs co-ordinator's ability to undertake the role and the school's capacity to change need careful planning. Dessent (1987) suggests that these changes can only develop over a period of time which might extend to several years. There is, therefore, much for special needs co-ordinators to learn from Georgiades and Phillimore's (1975) analysis of the change process and, in particular, from what they call the 'myth of the hero innovator'. They outline the pitfalls awaiting the innovator who, although fully committed and trained in all the theory, is doomed to fail in practice. If, they suggest, s/he fails to take account of the culture of the institution and of the interpersonal relationships and belief systems of individuals within it, or if s/he tries to change both him/herself and the institution at a stroke, then disaster beckons. Co-ordinators might well bear in mind Hopkins' (1987) dictum that organizations are sailed rather than driven.

What all of this points to is the need for long term planning that is paced to the ability of the institution to absorb the innovation into its own culture. Weightman (Thomas and Feiler 1988) argues for change that is planned in small steps, as it gives the opportunity to adjust, modify and reflect before continuing. *What is indicated, therefore, is a structured special needs development plan with realistic, achievable targets.* This must complement the school's development needs, otherwise it will lack support and little will be achieved.

Such consideration of pace is doubly important for its impact both on the whole school and on the personal resources of the co-ordinator. If what is attempted is too ambitious, the task will either intimidate some co-ordinators by its enormity or burn out others who attempt too much. Energy and commitment are essentials but, as Golby and Gulliver (1979) point out, these may not always have been channelled in the best direction. If, in the changing and troubled educational world of the 1990s, special needs co-ordinators do not direct their energies to long term goals which embed a vision of special needs provision in the culture of the school, they may end up achieving very little of lasting value.

The special needs co-ordinator's planning involves getting externally-generated values and policies on the school's agenda for action. *This can only be achieved by becoming professionally active within the whole school context.* This is especially difficult at a time of 'innovation fatigue', when mainstream teachers may be striving to maintain the *status quo* and be reluctant to change teaching strategies learned through trial and error over a number of years. Thus, any change must, as Steiner (1965) suggests, be perceived as new and better, and must be seen to bring direct benefits to the teachers who must implement it, or it will not be adopted.

It may be argued that this is too great a role for special needs co-ordinators as they are rarely members of senior management. However, the role of change agent in a school is not confined to the Head: a change agent is any individual who assumes a leadership role within a specific context. Of course, special needs co-ordinators need support in this role and some local education authorities build this into policy – as we shall shortly see in the case of Cheshire. Of equal importance, however, is the *status* they enjoy in the eyes of pupils, parents, colleagues and governors, as well as senior management. Such status is not conferred, it is earned – sometimes through charisma and energy, sometimes through professional credibility, but invariably reflecting a willingness to become involved in whole school issues.

Moreover, status, involvement and support are closely linked to the co-ordinator's ability to analyse where power lies in the school and to use it to develop special needs provision further. Power does not always lie with senior management. The co-ordinator should be aware of his/her own personal power, consider how to develop it, and use it constructively. Torrington, Weightman and Johns (1985) suggest that power emanates from:

- control of resources (i.e. what others need in terms of time, information, materials etc.)
- expertise
- motivation
- having others under obligation for past favours
- persuasion skills
- control of the agenda and
- charisma

Power, in other words, emanates from things that the co-ordinator does or could control; it does not necessarily arise from titles or pay.

All of this implies that the co-ordinator cannot look at how the institution might develop without also looking at him/herself in the context of that institution. Looking at oneself critically is a painful process, but *self-evaluation is the key to adopting the role of change agent*, and without personal knowledge there is no firm base on which to build and develop. Moreover, the appraisal process currently offers a promising focus for such self-evaluation and forward planning.

In particular, this implies that the co-ordinator:

- should undertake two levels of planning: personal and institutional – though these should reflect each other
- should have a personal development plan and
- should take responsibility for his/her own professional development within this plan.

The changes and innovations of the 1980s have provided some opportunities for this through in-service training (INSET), the Technical and Vocational Education Initiative (TVEI) and curriculum-based innovations. Beyond these, however, a personal development plan which reflects the dynamics of the school culture should 'test the market', asking:

- what does the school need?
- how can I provide it?
- how can I use this demand to further the cause of educational entitlement and meet pupil needs?

Such self-development is not simply about enhancing personal characteristics and qualities, but involves the acceptance of a behavioural component in the co-ordinator's role. It means, above all, becoming *proactive* – learning how to plan, how to avoid conflict and crisis management, how to work with and through 'key stimulators' in the school, and how to be opportunist, consultative and facilitative – how, in other words, to be considerably more sophisticated than the 'hero innovator'! Recent initiatives – in flexible learning, equal opportunities, records of achievement, appraisal, and the development of libraries as open learning or resources centres – provide special needs co-ordinators with unequalled chances to learn these skills. Above all, they can identify and utilize opportunities from within *existing* initiatives, rather than having to carry the whole burden of innovation themselves.

Working in this opportunistic way through existing initiatives has a number of advantages for special needs co-ordinators:

- it assists the co-ordinator's professional development
- it enhances the co-ordinator's status as an informed and credible member of the staff with wider emphasis than the traditional involvement with an atypical group of children
- it involves the co-ordinator in whole-school effective learning developments which involve planning, developing, monitoring and evaluating the educational provision for *all* children
- it extends responsibility for entitlement to a wider number of staff.

Some may still argue that the role of the special needs co-ordinator is to teach. However, *the role of the special needs co-ordinator is to promote learning.* Teaching is only one means whereby co-ordinators can achieve this, but as professionals they must seek to optimize learning by adopting a wider perspective, by planning and by examining their effectiveness. This is not an addition to teaching; it is at its heart. Effective learning results not simply from direct classroom intervention, but from a curriculum which takes account of individual differences, is adjusted to meet pupil needs and which is, therefore, planned and organized.

This notion forms the basis for much of the work undertaken by TVEI, focusing as it does on flexible teaching and learning and on the implicit values of equal opportunties. By being opportunistic, the special needs co-ordinator can influence classroom practice through the school's established TVEI work. Hence, not only are special needs developments seen as evolving from existing initiatives (thus not simply 'another change'), but they can utilize TVEI resources, groundwork and personnel. Above all, this work can evolve from what the staff and the school have *already* identified to be their needs. TVEI also gains by having a member of the school staff whose activities arise from a philosophy that is similarly based in curriculum entitlement and access. It is, in other words, a symbiotic relationship.

Development in action: the Cheshire experience

This was the starting point for a joint Cheshire Local Authority TVEI training initiative for special needs co-ordinators. The programme was planned to involve the high school special needs co-ordinators in three full days' training spread over a term. It focused on what were identified earlier in this chapter to be the co-ordinators' special needs, i.e. that training should be embedded in the microculture of the school and address a broadening of traditionally-expected professional and interpersonal skills. Moreover, since the co-ordinator needs senior management support, a mandate for the work was sought from the deputy heads with senior management responsibility for special needs. No co-ordinator could attend the training without the involvement of their deputy head in a pre-course meeting. The course organizers anticipated that they might have to be prepared for arguments concerning traditional withdrawal-*v*-learning support. Whilst the training was repeated three times, as Cheshire had, at that time, 72 high schools, this problem did not arise. There was, in fact, agreement between the deputy heads and the course organizers concerning a set of course aims:

- to enable the participants to manage their own changing role
- to promote the special needs co-ordinator as an agent for curriculum change and development within the school
- to facilitate evolution from a model of remediation to one of support
- to encourage participants to reflect on their own practice
- to encourage both a 'quality' and 'value added' component of the co-ordinator's role.

This was to be achieved by:

- enabling participants to identify their own needs for self-development
- establishing the essential issues in whole school approaches
- identifying the development needs of the school
- focusing on meeting the individual needs of pupils
- focusing on consultative and co-operative teaching strategies
- focusing on flexible learning management styles.

In order to develop further the dialogue between the deputy heads and their special needs co-ordinators, the focus of each training session was to be reported back to the deputy head.

It is not possible here to give more than an overview of the work that was undertaken. Certain key themes were addressed:

1. *The whole school implications of co-operative teaching and the consultative role.* Co-ordinators examined the implications for the subject teacher – in terms of classroom

management, teaching style and their existing perceptions of support – and for the support teacher – in terms of working with a larger number of pupils and negotiating a role reflecting the needs of both children and subject teacher. In order to encourage them to realize that each teacher could respond differently to these implications, they were asked to survey the attitudes of five colleagues who were perceived to possess some power in their institution.

2. *The development of interpersonal skills.* Because negotiation with colleagues plays an increasing part in the lives of co-ordinators, considerable time was allocated to allow them the opportunity to consider aspects of successful negotiation and communication.

3. *The advisory role.* Co-ordinators were assisted in producing a checklist of teaching and management options in language skills development for their school, followed by a menu of INSET activities that could be developed over a school year and be conducted at lunchtimes, in informal conversations, departmental meetings, special needs link group meetings, case conferences, or in curriculum groups. And in order to make sure something happened as a result of this, co-ordinators were asked to produce a programme for special needs INSET for the whole year and to negotiate this with the INSET co-ordinator – opportunistically identifying special needs components in already-planned INSET activities.

4. *Personal change.* A session was devoted to monitoring, self-evaluation and personal target setting with a systematic analysis as a planning tool. In order to ensure that the influence of the course was extended beyond its lifetime, the co-ordinators were asked to explain this systematic analysis to the deputy heads, and a joint session was arranged in which co-ordinators and deputies used the analysis to review and augment the schools' special needs development plan.

Inevitably every school involved in this training differed in how far it developed as a result of the course. Nevertheless, the county inspection programme has revealed that over the past three years there has been an increased sophistication in schools' interpretation of whole school approaches. Such a degree of development may not have occurred if special needs co-ordinators had not been assisted by the course to adopt the role of change agent.

Towards the year 2000

As change within the educational system continues at an unabated pace, the need for special needs co-ordinators to review and develop their role becomes acute. At the same time, the ability of local education authorities to support their co-ordinators in this process – as Cheshire has done – is under constant threat. I have argued in this chapter that the solution for co-ordinators is not to abandon their development but:

- to take responsibility for their own development
- to formulate an institutional special needs development plan
- to link this to a personal development plan based on self-evaluation
- to become active as change agents in the whole school context
- to establish status and power not through hierarchical position but through personal qualities and behaviours
- to become proactive and opportunistic in using existing initiatives.

This is a difficult and challenging undertaking. But co-ordinators who are successful, far from becoming a 'dying breed', will be in a position to play a major part in furthering notions of entitlement and equal opportunities in the schools of the next century.

References

Bines, H. (1986) *Redefining Remedial Education*. Beckenham: Croom Helm.

Butt, N. D. (1986) 'Implementing the whole school approach at secondary level', *Support for Learning*, 1(4), 10–15.

Butt, N. D. (1991) 'A role for the SEN co-ordinator in the 1990s: a reply to Dyson', *Support for Learning*, 6(1), 9–15

Department of Education and Science (1978) *Special Educational Needs (The Warnock Report)*. London: HMSO.

Dessent, T. (1987) *Making the Ordinary School Special*. Lewes: Falmer Press.

Dyson, A. (1990) 'Effective Learning Consultancy: a future role for special needs co-ordinators?', *Support for Learning*, 5(3), 16–27.

Dyson, A. (1991) 'Rethinking roles, rethinking concepts: special needs teachers in mainstream schools', *Support for Learning*, 6(2), 51–61.

Dyson, A. (1992) 'Innovatory mainstream practice: what's happening in schools' provision for special needs?', *Support for Learning*, 7(2), 51–62.

Georgiades, N. J. and Phillimore, L. (1975) 'The myth of the hero-innovator and alternative strategies for organizational change' reproduced in Easen, P. (1985) *Making School-centred INSET Work*. Beckenham: Croom Helm with the Open University.

Golby, M. and Gulliver, J. R. (1979) 'Whose remedies? Whose ills?', *Journal of Curriculum Studies*, 11(2), 137–147.

98

Hopkins, D. (1987) *Improving the Quality of Schooling.* London: Falmer Press.
Steiner, G. (1965) *The Creative Organization.* Chicago: University of Chicago Press.
Thomas, G. and Feiler, A. (1988) *Planning for Special Needs.* Oxford: Basil Blackwell.
Torrington, D., Weightman, J. and Johns, K. (1985) *Management Methods.* London: Institute of Personnel Management.

CHAPTER 9

Changing the School by Reflectively Re-defining the Role of the Special Needs Co-ordinator

Christine O'Hanlon

The one thing that has characterized teachers of pupils with special educational needs in the past has been their sense of mission, their unique view of pupils as individuals, and their conviction that the ordinary teacher in the school just does not have the time or the inclination to grapple with the total educational needs of special learners (Dyson 1991, O'Hanlon 1988). The expertise developed by these teachers in their years of successfully directing the energies of school pupils into individually productive practices has formed a wide body of information and experience in practice which has not only benefited schools but has also broadened the professional basis of the total teaching profession. The special needs teacher has supported pupils in their learning and teacher colleagues in their teaching by seeking to improve the matching of pupil's learning with professional's teaching.

On the other hand, the ordinary class teacher is generally coping with large classes and has great difficulty managing and teaching individual educational programmes for pupils who need individual tuition because of individual learning needs. Although it has often been stated that the term 'special educational needs' has outlived its usefulness, it is the one area which demands special and separate in-service training. This underlines the significance of the term and its function in the curriculum debate. In England and Wales initial teacher education, PGCE and B.Ed courses are required to provide students with basic knowledge and skills in the field of special educational needs. DES circular 24/89 lays down the principle that:

> Courses should prepare students for teaching the full range of pupils and for the diversity of ability, social background and

ethnic and cultural origin they are likely to encounter among pupils in mainstream schools.

However, there is evidence that the preparation of teachers is diverse and variable (DES 1989), and that the extent to which students in initial teacher education achieve any degree of specialization in special educational needs is a matter of debate (CNAA 1991). Hegarty and Moses (1988) claim that the awareness-raising nature of such courses is not sufficient. Since 1984, in England and Wales, the education of pupils with special educational needs requires a post experience qualification. It is considered essential for the special needs teacher to have enhanced professional status for their particular developmental needs. Their needs include expertise in special needs teaching, the management of innovation and resources, curriculum design and evaluation, home/school liaison and professional development with colleagues.

I would like to argue that the school's special educational needs teacher, whether designated the co-ordinator, the support teacher or the special needs teacher, is forced into a position of professional conflict because of the need to re-define the role within a changing school culture. The Education Reform Act (1988) has led to the implementation of the National Curriculum in England and Wales, and is complemented by the 5–14 Curriculum and Assessment programme and the 1990 regulations on national testing of pupils in P4 and P7 in Scotland. There are pilot schemes in the Delegated Management of Resources which are having the same effect on the in-service development of teachers as the Local Management of Schools (LMS) in England, Wales and Northern Ireland.

There has also been a move from segregated to mainstream education. In 1988 26% of pupils identified as having special needs were being educated in mainstream schools and the percentage in mainstream classes had risen to 16% (DES 1989). The majority of pupils referred to as having special educational needs do not have statements and the majority of pupils with statements are educated in special schools. Nevertheless there is a need to attend to the professional development needs of both the ordinary and the special school sector. In the ordinary school sector the sphere and influence of the special needs teacher is considerable and wide-ranging.

The Warnock Report (1978) established that 20% of all pupils could be considered to have special needs. In many ways this has led to a strengthening of general provision in the field of education for pupils with 'learning difficulties', or for pupils disaffected by schooling. Since 1978 there has been positive provision based on positive discrimination in favour of pupils with learning or school difficulties. Most of the new focus in the provision has been towards the fostering of in-school provision in the form of support teaching in the mainstream classroom. The person who has been most influential in the organization and management of this re-focusing has been the special needs teacher.

In the present educational climate, we might ask ourselves, 'What can an individual teacher do to influence policy and practice in a school? In particular, what can a teacher with specific responsibility for pupils with special educational needs do in the school context to bring about improvement for pupils in the wider school environment?' Teachers of special needs pupils have previously been relegated to the 'cupboard' or to the furthest mobile in the playground to get on with the inevitable task of advancing the literacy and numeracy skills of their charges, both in the primary and secondary sector. Now the opportunity presents itself to play an important role in mainstream education, and to influence the attitudes and values held by professionals in the competition for raising standards and attainment in the National Curriculum. They are now in a position to raise their status, make their voices heard, and deliberately to change the un-reflective practices in schools. They have the opportunity to become powerful change agents. The manipulation of power or changing the structure of the school has not normally been conceived by them as a fruitful endeavour because it has not been within their grasp. Yet there have been major changes made within schools recently that have been influenced by the 'special needs culture' of the school. Influenced in two senses, one by the person who organizes the special needs department or is known as the 'remedial' or 'withdrawal' or 'support' teacher, the other is the influence of the wider structural and organizational changes related to integration ie., Warnock and the 1981 Act versus Education Reform Act (1988) and the National Curriculum which includes local management of schools (LMS) and its implications.

Whatever changes take place in the school inevitably affect the education of pupils with special educational needs. Forms of practice vary from school to school where there is always the dilemma of whether or not to disguise the number of special needs pupils in order to bring the financial benefit of increased enrolment, or whether to exaggerate the numbers in order to attract more funds from the local authority.

The inquiring practitioner

I have personally been involved in the management of change with many mainstream special needs teachers in recent years, as a result of which I have gained a greater understanding of the nature of control and power within schools and the teacher's role in the process. The teachers have spent between two and three years on a part-time degree course engaged in the active investigation, reflection and improvement of practices in schools related to special needs pupils. The underlying philosophy of the course is professional development through action research. The means of allowing teachers control over their own learning or professional development, of understanding their values, developing their own meanings through educational inquiry, of self-direction, and the analysis of the what and how they come to know, has been variously referred to as reflective inquiry, reflective practice, action research and critical enquiry. The main aim of such enquiry is to question specific assumptions underlying the school as a community, for example the function of social control, and the meaning of such terms as responsibility, opportunity, merit and ability.

As a form of teacher education critical qualitative research becomes a mode of learning. It provides the foundation for significant and worthwhile change in individual and institutional teacher education. The individual, as a result of research and reflective practice, becomes a more confident thinker. This thinking, which creates action planning, is linked to the teacher's personal understanding of professional effectiveness. The individual cannot escape becoming self-aware and self-evaluative through the process of professional change based on reflective practice (Schön [1987], Elliott [1973], and Stenhouse [1975]).

Teachers who are engaged in educational research are making judgements about the orientation of their research, they are drawing boundaries between what is acceptable, and what is not in their schools. They are making judgements about the efficacy and effectiveness of certain practices in teaching, for example, withdrawal teaching or in-class support. They are using their power to promote, follow up and investigate particular views of educational excellence and failure. They are questioning the ideological basis of certain educational practices. In this activity they create and constitute the ideological dimension within the act of inquiry which models a form of democratic evaluation. The researcher uses his/her power to change the existing practice in the school, therefore the ideological balance inherent in the practice also becomes affected by the changes.

Teacher researchers often make the mistake of assuming that power is always consciously exercised by a cabal of conspirators seeking to control the educational world (Kincheloe 1991). Teachers are prevented from acting deliberately and in a proactive way when they believe that there is a school hierarchy of command which cannot be influenced. Critical inquiry within the school empowers the teacher researcher, in that it allows the special needs teacher to share evidence, discuss issues and to engage in reflective decision making with colleagues.

What is the significance of qualitative research for special needs provision in mainstream schools and what is the implication for future professional development?

The special needs co-ordinator

This is best related to the basic understanding of the role of the special needs co-ordinator. Dyer (1988) asserts that support implies intervention strategies at the point of delivery where teaching and learning meet.

However, any form of support implies a shift in thinking about the educational needs of learners. Our present views rest on a revised view of pupils which includes:

a) the recognition of the right of all pupils to a common education
b) the development of a broad and balanced curriculum
c) alternative ways of organizing access to the curriculum for low achievers.

The support available within the school may be applied to:

1) individuals or groups of pupils

2) professional resources and colleagues
3) classroom teaching and delivery.

This may in practice take many forms, for example, consultation, preparation, remediation, diagnosis, withdrawal, observation and classroom delivery.

The implications are that the school 'support' teacher is trained, flexible, skilled and proficient in the management, teaching, planning and organization of the curriculum for both individuals and groups of pupils.

If this is the co-ordinator's role, then s/he lives a nomadic school existence and depends on his/her wits and ability to respond flexibly to the demands of changing classroom contexts. Therefore the role is essentially an emergent role because:

- unlike most teaching roles, it is a negotiated role
- the conditions of the role depend upon the specific circumstances within the school
- there is no identifiable pupil group for teacher-pupil bonding
- the main support resources lie within the teacher
- it is similar to the peripatetic teacher's role, but within the school
- responsibility for pupils is transferred to the wider school context i.e. individual responsibility for individual pupils is diminished
- initiation of teamwork is essential to the democratic balance of teaching in the classroom
- territorial rights are to be bargained for.

Although the co-ordinator is relying on his/her personal resources as a basis for professional practice, s/he nevertheless is in a position to communicate with a large number of the staff in consultation about the delivery of the curriculum. We can make the claim that

> The special needs co-ordinator is in a powerful position to change the structure and practice within the school, or that the co-ordinator will need to be strong and develop powerful means of asserting his/her influence on the situation if the role is to develop further.

Both the special needs co-ordinator and the ordinary teacher experience change in their role and practice in the move towards support teaching, but the negotiation and sharing within the classroom depends largely on the generosity and flexibility of the class teacher. The special needs teacher, in moving into the ordinary classroom, is in occupied territory. The classroom is resourced, defined, and organized by the class or subject teacher. Also the lesson content relates to the class teacher's syllabus which may be fixed i.e. the National Curriculum. Therefore there will be a considerable variety of procedure and support practised on the intervention of the special needs co-ordinator. This complex role can only be developed by barter, negotiation and compromise on both the part of the special needs co-ordinator and the class teacher.

The inclination is to try to simplify the complexity of such a situation to make it manageable and understandable. We are dealing with personal emotion and feeling related to the special needs professional's loss of dominion, loss of a focus of power, loss of control, loss of professional autonomy, loss of private space, loss of a stable base, loss of tradition, continuity and familiarity.

There is also the uncertainty, emotion and feeling surrounding making new collegial alliances, exposing expertise to others, asserting rights of practice in shared classrooms, and offering a quality of service to pupils which is genuinely helpful and educational.

Process of change and redefinition

Both the special needs co-ordinator and the ordinary teacher are in a process of change which offers the opportunity for bargaining, for the re-negotiation of roles and practices, and for the special needs co-ordinator to influence mainstream classroom practices and assert his/her particular educational values and practices. Thinking of practice as an activity that underlines theory is important in bringing about change in the practices of schools and teaching. The argument about changing roles is not one of change-*v*-stasis. It is about the extent to which teachers involve themselves in the dialogue of school practice. It is about special needs teachers taking control of their own school practices with an understanding of their theoretical origins and ideological emphases. Taking control of the origins and ideologies which direct activities involve reflection on practices and a conscious awareness of the factors in situations that are of personal value in schools. Teachers must find a means of articulating their theory/understanding in a manner which causes debate and fosters communication of the issues related to their values among their colleagues. Critical equiry or action research does not simply provide practitioners with ready made solutions to problems in practice, but to renewed means of thinking and meaning related to teaching and learning. Fresh thinking about issues related to pupils with learning difficulties in schools is context related and variable. It depends on many complex social factors in the situation, for example the teachers' previous learning and experience, their values, attitudes and perceptions, the situational or school ethos, the learning and experience of other colleagues, and their values, attitudes and perceptions.

Our aim as educators and researchers is to understand what our personal position is within ideologies and within institutions and to know how it limits our vision of pupils and schools. We must become aware of our own ideological inheritance and its influence on our belief and value structures, our interests, and our practices in our professional lives. Social visions of educating all pupils with special educational needs to their potential within the school curriculum are not enough. Selden (1984) in his analysis of ideology in educational research shows how social visions shaped eugenicist research design. The visions of civilization, human progress and a good society were linked to the development of eugenicist research. He notes the irony of the fact that the instruments devised by eugenicist researchers to measure learning, intelligence, and ability are still employed in modern education. There is the further irony that within schools it is the special educational needs co-ordinator who is considered to hold the expertise in the testing and assessment of individual pupils. The low status which is conferred on the special needs teacher who purveys the technological results of high status knowledge can be exchanged for a higher status by the redefinition of the role in schools. In redefining the role it is essential to develop and sustain the existing stock of professional knowledge built up over the years. The best way to achieve this and to develop the political dimension of special educational needs related to the issues of equal access to the curriculum, forms of assessment in the curriculum etc., *is to find a means to enable collaborative and critical inquiry within the schools.* The inquiring role could be combined with the teaching role and formally incorporated into the school development plan or the professional development programme within the school or the local authority. In exposing the educational purposes and values within the school in the process of action research, the justifications for the eduational policies on which they are based are also exposed. These are fundamentally political institutional issues which invariably provide the conditions for conflict when one challenges or attempts to change them.

Polan (1989) sees conflict at the very centre of the process of institutional organization, which may be seen as an essential set of procedures for members to explore the possible acceptance or rejection of new solutions to changing educational problems. He suggests the only alternative is for institutions to develop a process of *open* communication through information exchange, debate, reflection, conflict and consensus through conflict, or decisions based on the widest available information.

The implication is that there is a role in every school for the 'reflective practitioner' to address the tension existing at present between directives from the high ground, which are being put into practice by the concerned practitioners in the swampy lowland (Schön 1987).

Schön also stresses the impossibility of professional advancement in individuated contexts without some form of reflective practice:

> If we focus on the kinds of reflection-in-action through which practitioners sometimes make new sense of uncertain, unique or conflicted situations of practice, then we will assume neither that existing professional knowledge fits every case nor that every problem has a right answer.

It is the role of future educators, particularly those of us concerned about the future status of pupils with special educational needs and their specially trained and experienced teachers, to engage in reflective conversations about the dominance of knowledge-based ideologies in the schools and to engage in a dialogue with colleagues at all levels to re-interpret the resultant repercussions of existing ideologies aimed at control of teachers through the control of pupils. The micro-politics of the school are being constantly reformed by the individual and collective interests of teachers and pupils (Ball 1987).

The future role of special needs co-ordinators depends upon their view of themselves as capable of proactive intervention in

108

the active and planned reconstruction of the school's response to the present threats implicit in the new legislation. This view can be developed by allowing the autonomous and critical inquiry of special needs professionals in schools, by supporting a form of professional development involving reflective practice. It is only by emphasising the competence, proficiency and expertise of special needs co-ordinators and increasing their potential for 'reflective situational decision making' in the schools that they will become powerful and transform the wider education culture. When special needs co-ordinators promote reflective educational practice and encourage colleagues to enquire into their practical understanding of educational situations, when they develop collaborative research activities into the school's policy and practice in the education of *all* pupils, then the school culture will be transformed by their intervention. The special needs teacher must become powerful through the practice of negotiation, of improving and changing classroom practice based on evidence that is shared, discussed and deliberated upon. A shared reflective practice may, however, lead to compromises.

Elliott writes:

> It is naïve to assume that Government alone has the power to shape academic and practical cultures within society. Social change in democracies is usually in practice, if not in intention, a matter of negotiated compromises and trade-offs. (Elliott, 1991)

The situation is one that needs more inter-professional investigation in the area that most concerns us i.e., the inclusion and the teaching of all pupils in an environment that promotes their potential for learning, and their equal opportunity to display and expand their natural abilities in schools. The in-service provision of teachers must address the needs of special learners and encourage schools to become 'reflective schools' by the active intervention of critical and reflective inquirers. Professional development must include the practical evaluation of professional practice by practitioners in schools. The role of the College or University is to direct the process towards institutional sustainability.

References

Ball, S. (1987) *The Micro-Politics of the School: Towards a Theory of School Organisation*. London: Methuen.

Council for National Academic Awards (1991) *Review of Special Educational Needs in Initial and Inservice Teacher Education Courses.* London.

Department of Education and Science (1989) *Statistics of Education: Schools 1988* (Circular 24/89).

Department of Education and Science (1978) *Special Educational Needs (The Warnock Report).* London: HMSO.

Dyer, C. (1988) 'Which support? An examination of the term', in *Support for Learning,* **3**, 1. 6−11.

Dyson, A. (1991) 'Rethinking roles, rethinking concepts: special needs teachers in mainstream schools' in *Schools for Learning.* **6**, 2, 51−61.

Elliott, J. (1973) 'Reflecting where the action is: the design of the Ford teaching project' in *Education for Teaching.* November 8−20.

Elliott, J. (1991) *Three Perspectives on Coherence and Continuity* in teacher education paper presented at UCET Annual Conference, November.

Hegarty, S. & Moses, D. (eds.) (1988) *Developing Expertise: Inset for Special Educational Needs.* Windsor: NFER-Nelson.

Kincheloe, J.L. (1991) *Teachers as Researchers: qualitative enquiry as a path to improvement.* London: Falmer.

O'Hanlon, C. (1988) 'Alienation within the profession: special needs or watered down teachers? Insights into the tension between the ideal and the real through action research' in *Cambridge Journal of Education* **18**, 3, 297−312.

Polan, A. (1989) School, 'The inevitable democracy?' in *The Democratic School,* Harber, C. & Meighan, R. (eds) Education, New Publishing Co-Op Ltd. Ticknall.

Selden, S. (1984) 'Objectivity and Ideology in Educational Research'. *Phi Delta Kappan* **66**, 4, 281−3.

Schön, D. (1987) *Educating The Reflective Practitioner.* San Francisco: Jossey-Bass.

Stenhouse, L. (1975) *An Introduction to Curricular Research and Development.* London: Heinemann.

CHAPTER 10

Gritty, Sensible and Utilitarian – the Only Model?: Special Educational Needs Initial Teacher Training and Professional Development

David Thomas

To start a piece on teacher education and training two weeks before a General Election, where the parties have differing education agendas, could mean an approach that is either ultra cautious or romantically unrealistic. Given the pace and volume of change within education, especially since 1987, it is highly likely that anyone writing *then* would have forecast the cumulative impact of an Education Reform Act with its National Curriculum, national assessment, the paving of the way towards subject specialisms in primary schools, the return of paper and pencil examinations as the course work proportion is diminished and the Local Management of Schools. Nor could one have foreseen emasculated local educational authorities, a hobbled HM Inspectorate, the threat of teacher redundancies within and without rate-capped authorities, the eradication of the binary divide, the prospects of higher education's massive expansion within limited resources and, most pertinently, the radical proposals for teacher training where much of the student's time will be spent in schools. What I am saying is, I could get it wrong and probably will.

Education and Training

The longstanding dichotomy between education and training has not lost any of its potency through its longevity. The flavour of the distinction between the two terms is neatly captured by Furnham comparing the teaching and training of undergraduates with those of managers. Students on academic courses are, he claims, taught 'theory, first principles and abstract understanding'. Managers' training is 'practical and concrete ... gritty, sensible ... and utilitarian'.

> Background details, historical origins and theoretical models give way to practical understanding and doing skills. 'Training effectiveness' is the speed by which people can acquire and practise relevant skills, not the extent to which they understand theoretical concepts. (Furnham, 1992.)

This is precisely the dilemma of the teacher trainer: the extent to which time-limited programmes can balance the interactive claims of principles and practice. Between the cautious, critical, academic stance and the messianic certainties of those promoting their personal convictions as to solutions to difficult problems, lies an immense gulf: one of approach, content, style and ideology.

The shape, texture and coloration of teacher training is contested. The debate includes those wishing a return to a pupil-teacher model with its intention of preventing new teachers from acquiring dangerous educational dogma from university departments of education; the Licensed Teacher scheme to allow the unqualified into the profession and that other variant, the Articled Teacher scheme. It also includes the Council for the Accreditation of Teacher Education (CATE) branding-iron model (Circulars 3/83 and 24/89) with its increasing specificity of training outcomes eventuating in a competence model explicitly derived (ideologically) from industrial practices and the 'teaching hospital model' favoured by David Hargreaves and some of his colleagues at Cambridge (Beardon *et al*, 1992). As counter-weight there are those who advocate the retention of teacher training but removing from it repellent lefty tendencies and replacing these with an intellectually stimulating diet of history, philosophy, psychology and spavined sociology while simultaneously arguing that 'no one can be taught to teach'. Occupying an increasingly narrow strip of ground against the rising tide of the de-intellectualizing of teacher education are the brave but depleted cohort fighting under the tattered banner of reflective praxis. (Marsden, 1992.)

This is not the place to enter into the debate on whether students in initial training should be regarded as trainee instructors or professional apprentices and paid accordingly, within a training system which centres upon 'training schools'. Current practices already contain a balanced regime of training institution in-put and school-based experience (Beardon *et al*, 1992, Barret *et al*,

1992). Whether a government of a different complexion will alter earlier proposals that schools should play a much larger part in initial training and that training should be competences driven remains to be seen (DES 1992). A guess would be that the movement towards school-focused training is here to stay although whether it will be the 80/20% division is still negotiable.

The rest of this paper makes certain assumptions: that school-focused training will be the norm; that competences will be the measure of professional socialization and that resources, through devolved budgets, for long-term professional development of teachers will increasingly be controlled by schools, including governing bodies through devolved funding. The other major assumption is that special educational needs will be a Cinderella dimension, attracting to it marginalized teachers as well as marginalized pupils. There is insufficient space to address the content of special needs training so the emphasis will be upon its contexts.

It is not possible to consider the training needs of special educators without attempting to understand or guess at some of the possible outcomes of a school-focused initial training. Her Majesty's Inspectors were clear that there was a core of professional study-experience-reflection which was the *student's* experience of schools and teaching. Through this process it would provide students:

> ... with an understanding of the ways children develop and learn (especially language and number), the principles and practices of assessment; individual differences in the way in which children learn, with understanding of the more common learning difficulties.... (p. 10)

This passage concludes with the sentiment that training should:

> ... enable him [*sic*] to place his work within a broader framework of educational meaning and purpose, as well as contributing to his own powers of reasoning, clear thought and expression so that he may aid the development of these capacities in the children he teaches. (DES, 1983)

Again, we have here an expression of the difficulty of seeing education both as a broad function for the whole of professional life with the need to prepare students for their more immediate participation in school and classroom activities but with the clear intention that both theory and practice were not only inter-related but derived from students' classroom and school experiences. It argued for a balanced approach but was clear that what it called the 'professional element' should be taught by successful and experienced teachers who were 'up-to-date in their knowledge of schools and society'. Their function was to develop in students an informed empirical approach to teaching tasks.

The success of higher education training institutions in providing appropriate preparation for pre-service teachers to meet special needs has been variable. They have found themselves, for a variety of reasons, coping with this problem through either ghetto-izing special needs into strictly cabined timetable slots (often using imported experts) or relying on a diffusion model in which the quality control over subject specialist tutors' input was at best partial and at worse, non-existent.

In this respect it may be anticipated that initial teacher training [ITT], which is largely school-based and definitely school-focused, ought to be able to play a very positive role in preparing students to identify and meet individual pupils' individual learning needs. After all, experienced teachers dealing with mixed ability groupings should be able to help the student not only with practical advice on the selection and pacing of curriculum content and delivery but also with the centrally important areas of class management skills and the development of good personal relationships which are the *sine qua non* for successful practice with pupils with learning difficulties. Extended contact over two teaching practices will enable students to form good working relationships with their pupils and have the time to experience the special rewards which come from helping a pupil over a learning hurdle.

However, the success of such a venture clearly depends upon evolving *modus operandi* between schools and training institutions. When the school-based training movement initiative was mooted, the language was one of partnership. Increasingly, the simple partition of schools doing the practical bit and higher education doing the theory end is challenged by recent innovatory experiences. (Booth *et al*, 1991). McIntyre draws attention to three phases in initial training: the technical level (effective attainment of selected targets), the practical level, where the assumptions, predispositions and consequences of actions are linked and the third level which is termed critical or emancipatory, where global issues of an ethical, social or political nature are considered. Central to the phases is the development of students' critical reflections on their own practices after they have achieved a minimal level of classroom competence. In the Oxford programme phase one is devoted to acquiring basic skills (getting and keeping classroom order, purposeful activities, gaining and keeping pupils' attention). Phase two is given over to practical reflectivity.

> We find it necessary to distinguish these two phases for three main reasons. First, mentors would ... be properly impatient with an emphasis on student-teachers exploring the implication for classroom practice of their own educational values before they had attained a minimal classroom competence. Second, most student teachers themselves lack the concern or the confidence to work through the implications of their ideals until they have first assured themselves that, in the eyes of their mentors and tutors, they are 'all right', competent and 'can do the job'. Third, it takes two-thirds of the year before most student-teachers have learned enough about the complexities of classroom teaching to be able meaningfully to attempt to relate their classroom practice to their educational values. (McIntyre, 1991.)

This draws our attention to what is realistically possible in a one year post graduate course as a general preparation for teaching and the limits to what may be expected in the way of producing novice teachers ready to deal with special needs. The very positive aspect is that sound, general principles of good teaching learned under the sensitive guidance of both mentor and tutor provide a substantive contribution towards the acquisition and development of those skills and attitudes needed to respond to special educational needs. It is also sociologically sound that meeting special needs should grow out of contact with such pupils within a mainstream setting; that is, meeting special needs is a regular part of teaching.

Competence model

If, as seems plausible, the assessment of students' professional progress is premised upon performance indicators, then the quality of special needs training will depend on the prominence of these in the competences profile used by training institutions and their partner schools. Professional preparation will be driven by the assessment profile. Among stated aims for the new training model – understanding the subject, ability to produce lesson plans, providing curriculum continuity and progression and presenting subject content in clear language and in a stimulating manner – are two aims directly relevant to special educational needs. They are the ability to set appropriately demanding expectations and to employ a range of strategies appropriate to the age, ability and level of pupil (DES Consultation Document, 2.3.3. and 2.3.4; 1992).

If students in initial training are well tutored in these areas it might be hoped that such instruction would provide a sound basis for the start of professional development moving on to increasing confidence and competence in curriculum planning, delivery and assessment based on insights into needs. If much needed skills such as these are ingrained they will need to be placed within a cognitive and social frame which produces understandings of the causes, symptoms and circumstances which facilitate disadvantage, discrimination and low-expectations. It is at this level the training institutions will still have much to contribute although, under optimum conditions, such a background of ideas will be informed by valid classroom and school experiences. Phase two is as vital as the first phase.

The National Curriculum and special needs

The student will function within a school culture that has been transformed by the Education Reform Act and particularly by the National Curriculum. Of the latter, one of the significant features of its development has been the tendency to place the needs of the academically able pupil first. The (initially) much vaunted 'entitlement for all' philosophy was revealed as distortion of its real socio-political aims. The stated political motive for the National Curriculum was the arrest of falling standards. The higher levels of the grading system were designed to pull up the performance of the abler pupils.

It should be remembered that Level Four is the base of the new GCSE ... the range of work required for this level is considerable. Not many seven-year-olds will have mastered decimal notation to two places or the relationship between the sun and the phases of the moon as well as writing independently with accurate sentence punctuation. The way that the Standard Attainment Tasks (SATS) are structured, the pressure from parents and the need for schools and local authorities to perform well in league tables will probably conspire to ensure that a reasonable minority will reach this standard. From then on their progress is assured.... Bright children will be propelled through an information-heavy curriculum rooted in reading and writing ... the outcome will be a handful of Mensa recruits, an even larger number of academic drop-outs and a vast number of individuals who feel classified as failures. (Sweetman, 1992)

While, in the early days, teachers in mainstream and special schools worked doggedly to develop schemes of work which could work alongside and complement that taking place within the National Curriculum, the more recent curriculum developments and allocation of resources have made life more difficult. (Ashdown *et al*, 1991.) The increasing use of paper and pencil tests at the key stages will disenfranchise many pupils with learning difficulties. The pressure to re-introduce whole-class teaching, subject specialisms in the primary schools will produce an underclass of failures: those who at Key Stage 1 will be designated as 'Level W' pupils — those working towards Level 1 — with the danger of being labelled the 'Wally' Level. The educational resource devoted to the bottom 20% has always been one of the smallest and the most vulnerable in times of economic limitations. The impact of financial difficulties upon integration schemes heavily dependent upon the use of support teachers in the classroom is likely to be severe.

All these factors combine to reinforce an educational culture in which resources and rewards go to the ablest and the least able are liable to get such crumbs as compassion may allow. So much for entitlement!

In-service training

Until recently, much in-service activity has been National Curriculum related and much organized around school-focused, subject-specific curriculum or assessment work. Recent reports have drawn attention to the danger of incestuous school-based in-service with its danger of re-cycled bad practice and the value of in-service training provision drawing on expertise from outside the school and off-site. But counter to this, as new National Curriculum subjects come on-stream, there will be a continuing resource-hungry demand for training in these subjects. The 'value for money concept' in in-service training could mean an increasing emphasis upon skills-related training with easily measurable outcomes with little room for courses of a more flexible character. Schools with grant maintained status are likely to have a budget of £40 per pupil for all Education Support Grant spending. The question arises whether schools in the new climate will feel spending money on special needs training is value for their money.

Continuing Professional Development

Beyond initial teacher training professional development requirement is recognized in induction schemes for probationary year teachers where the inputs of school mentors and higher education tutors is supplemented and complemented. It is here, following successful mastery of the basic mechanics of teaching, that new teachers will feel more confident about extending their experience to cope with pupils presenting signs of learning difficulties. A really powerful national induction programme would be a sound educational investment.

Beyond initial teacher training and induction is the territory of teachers' professional development. Surveying this particular landscape is to see the absence of clearly marked routes and staging posts. The professional experiences of teachers in the last few years have been in the nature of emergency rescue packs, survival kits on assessment at Key Stage 1, curriculum planning in Science Key Stages 1 and 2, reporting to parents etc. All of these are vital to functional survival in the classroom but not part of a well-thought-out scheme of professional and personal growth. The problems this creates are particularly acute in the special needs domain. At one time there was a clear route through one-year and term courses which could lead to Masters courses. This route provided a channel for future leaders in the field. Such routes are still in place but not all interested teachers can take full advantage of available opportunities. Two illustrations: a teacher attending a one-day conference which had a further one-day follow-up meeting stated she could not attend the second session but a colleague from her school would attend since the school's budget only ran to one one-day in-service training per member of staff and this was shared out equally. Second, a comment by an M.Ed admissions tutor points out the preponderance of TINCs in a new intake − Two Incomes, No Children. Access to higher education is increasingly conditional upon self-funding: appropriate for a monetarist era but hardly a suitable way of furthering the professional development of teachers.

Professional development in the future

This bleak but not unrealistic picture of professional development I need to offset with some positives, in addition to those which will come eventually from school-focused initial training and induction schemes. The first concerns the local authority and particularly its advisory and support services. It is now understood, even at the Department for Education, that some services to schools, teachers and pupils are better delivered from a central source. There are local authorities who are determined to maintain a supportive presence and where strenuous attempts are being made to ensure the survival of teacher development centres where in-service training, finely tuned to local needs, can be delivered. Partnership structures with Higher Education can ensure a measure of supported access to professional development. At the moment this relationship is one with elements of competitiveness as well as partnership but both must recognize that the long-term interests of teachers are better defended by a dialogical relationship. One of the urgent tasks for higher education is to find ways of accrediting teachers' experiences to give them appropriate advanced standing on award bearing courses.

The second positive aspect comes from the moral professionalism of teachers. I sense that while their attention has been and is diverted to the pressing concerns of National Curriculum delivery and its assessment, they have not lost sight of their pastoral and pedagogic responsibilities to disadvantaged pupils. In spite of all the pressures on schools to focus upon their communities and local authority ranking, there are teachers who will not abandon the gains made through integration and whole-school policies and they require support from both local authorities and higher education. If head teachers, from understandable motives, are preventing notices of special needs (and other) in-service training opportunities from reaching their staffroom, there are teachers willing and able to find their own sources of information and to make their professional demands known.

The fact that teachers are willing to fund themselves on to advanced courses is convincing evidence of their commitment to the special needs area. This moral professionalism will also ensure that pupils with learning difficulties will receive an appropriate entitlement curriculum although this will not be easy to achieve.

Higher education and local authority providers will continue to wrestle with interaction of general and abstract ideas with gritty, sensible, utilitarian classroom imperatives. In times of acute pressure the latter come into prominence but sooner or later there is the need to develop a perspective. A position and even a philosophy emerge and the question changes from 'What do I do with this child?', to 'Why am I doing this to this child'?

In my view, education and training to improve the meeting of special needs should be structured around the idea of raising the effectiveness of schools as responsive systems to provide a counter-balance to the former, excessive, individualization of both problems and solutions (Ainscow 1991). The needs of the individual teacher and her pupil are conceptualized within a systematic frame in which individualization is regarded as potentially a case-study for institutional change.

Between the pressures on schools to be reactive to externally imposed changes on their practices and the resistance of moral professionalism to inappropriate demands lies the future of special educational needs. In other words, its future is, to a large extent, within the choices schools make. Those of us on the margins of such decisions can encourage and support the resistive processes.

References

Ainscow, M. (1991) 'Towards effective schools for all', in Upton, G. (ed) *Staff Training and Special Educational Needs*. London: David Fulton.

Ashdown, R., Carpenter, B. and Bovair, K. (eds) (1991) *The Curriculum Challenge: Access to the National Curriculum for pupils with learning difficulties*. London: Falmer Press.

Barret, E. *et al* (1992) *Initial Teacher Education in England and Wales: A topography*. London: Goldsmiths College.

Beardon, T., Booth, M., Hargreaves, D. and Reiss, M. (1992) *School-led Initial Teacher Training*. Cambridge: DES.

Booth, M., Furlong, J. and Wilkin, M. (eds) (1991) *Partnership in Initial Training* London: Cassell.

Department of Education and Science (1983) *Teaching in Schools: The content of initial teacher training*. London: HMI.

Department of Education and Science (1992) *Reform of Initial Teacher Training: a consultation document*. London: DES.

Furnham, A. (1992) 'A time to teach and a time to learn' ... *New Scientist*, **1813**, 21 March, 51 – 2

Graves, N. (ed) (1991) *Initial Teacher Education: policies and progress*. London: Kogan Page.

Marsden, W. (1990) *W(h)ither Initial Teacher Education?* Department of Education Seminar. University of Liverpool.

McIntyre, D. (1991) *Theory, Theorizing and Reflection in Initial Teacher Education,* Paper presented at the Conceptualizing Reflective Teaching Conference, University of Bath.

Sweetman, J. (1992) 'Turning up the Brightness', *Education Guardian,* 10 March, 23.

CHAPTER 11

How Will the 'Self-Managing School' Manage?

John Moore

The role of the local education authority

As regards the future of the local education authority current wisdom would suggest that there are at least three scenarios. The local authority will, as the Audit Commission predicted (1989), find a new role in strategic and quality assurance functions and thereby facilitate a community based approach to local management; or it will systematically strip itself of layers of responsibility, handing these over to schools on a carefully planned and supported basis retaining, as Coopers and Lybrand Deloitte (1992) suggest, some elements of strategic planning, provision of information and a limited number of direct services to pupils, students and parents; or it will, through further legislation find itself without any real ground for being as regional bodies take over what statutory duties remain.

Whatever the outcome, the immediate and intermediate goal of the local education authority remains as Sayer (1987) and subsequently others have suggested, that schools should accommodate individual difference. This will take some considerable time to achieve and whilst the route may be uncertain, the vehicle is not. Much has been said and written about the destructive tendencies of local management for meeting special eduational needs, but the logic of the development of the self-managing school, if it is allowed its fullest realization is 'the school for all'. That this could be achieved more speedily by devolving decision-making processes to schools is, at least for this local authority officer, an uncomfortable proposition, but one nevertheless held as true.

Whilst the long term future of the local education authority may be open to question, the short and medium term is less so. There are irresistible forces shaping the role of the local authority which will not be re-focused by changes in national or local government. It is a political fact of life that local management has caught the imagination of councillors of all persuasions and that governors and head teachers welcome the opportunity to exercise fiscal power over the running of their schools. Even where opting-out is not an issue, local authorities will find it increasingly difficult to resist the ever growing demands of schools for greater devolution of local authority controlled budgets. The role of the local authority, beyond statutory duties, will depend to some considerable extent on those services its schools wish it to deliver.

Some authorities have already begun to examine the implications of this trend for the delivery of statutory services and there is increasing concern that there will be insufficient resources available to carry out these duties. One authority, for example, has examined all of its functions under three headings; black, white and grey. Black represents statutory functions such as those required by the Education Act 1981. White represents functions that could be provided by other agencies, such as those linked to in-service education and training and peripatetic special needs support to non-statemented pupils. Grey represents functions which could be provided by others but for which there would be good reason to maintain a local authority 'arms-length' services, such as advice and support for National Curriculum subjects.

In planning services local authorities have become increasingly aware of the fragility of those services operating outside of the structure of local management. Where the majority of schools are locally managed within an authority, for example, special schools have been quick to realize the frailty of their budgets. Likewise, a number of special needs support services have not survived the setting of a local authority budget. Capping and budgeting within the Standard Spending Assessment has meant that many local authorities have cut central services rather than risk the confidence of locally managed schools. The balance of uncertainty has swung from locally managed providers to local authority managed providers. This has made special educational needs an extremely vulnerable business, one least likely to survive outside of the framework of local management.

As Moore (1991) suggests, however, the arcane procedures required by the Education Act 1981 conspire against the successful devolution of responsibility for special needs. The Act places the local authority at the centre of decision-making and most commentators appear to agree that this is unhelpful. Centralized control of assessment and resource allocation is a legacy of the Warnock Committee's view that special educational needs require resources which are additional or supplementary to provision normally made by schools. This concept does not hold good for self-management. Such a view perpetuates a division between those pupils with a Statement and those without, thus encouraging segregation. If the concept of the self-managing school is to mean anything for special educational needs then it must assist in the destruction of this demarcation. This would seem a prerequisite to translating special educational needs into the more inclusive concept of individual difference.

A model more consistent with local management would ensure that decisions are made close to the neighbourhood of the child and in a way that involves a wide group of professionals in partnership with parents and pupils. This will require a sophisticated mechanism, one which links an in-school review of pupil needs to a community based assessment, where the community based assessment replaces the 1981 Act procedures. The advantage of such a mechanism would be to remove the barrier between statemented and non-statemented pupils, offering self-managing schools the opportunity to respond to educational needs as a community. This would require a re-working of current special needs designations into levels of support and a description of one local authority's attempt to do this appears below.

The construction and maintenance of such a mechanism is, it could be argued, the medium term role of the local authority. It would prevent the decline into a free-market oriented response, which inevitably, if left unchecked, will create an inconsistent and incoherent response to needs. The strategic function of the local authority therefore, is the construction and servicing of a mechanism which enables locally managed schools to meet needs within a community. The quality assurance role, whilst somewhat diminished by the Schools Bill (1992), remains. Its twin objectives of informing resource allocation and organizational patterns (Moore, 1991) continue to be at the heart of policy formulation and strategic thrust. Inspection is but one part of quality assurance, a privatized inspectorate cannot offer the local authority total quality control. The concept of total quality control is as relevant to the local authority as it is to every self-managing institution. It is the examination and improvement of every process which impinges upon the child's experiences of success or failure within the curriculum. However special educational needs are viewed, as under-achievement, individual difference or educational needs, total quality control will emerge as one of the fundamental tenets of successful self-management.

Locally-managed resources

That locally-controlled resources is a fundamental aspect of meeting special educational needs within the mainstream is well explored by Thomas (1992). Thomas, however, dismisses a role for the local authority which he sees as still essentially centralist and bureaucratic, arguing instead for direct funding of all pupil needs, and therefore direct responsibility and accountability to schools. Thomas's basic assumption is that local authorities perpetuate the notion of services, which in turn de-skill by generating a culture of dependency. In essence this is much the same argument which Moore and Morrison (1988) have made, that meeting special eduational needs will remain 'someone else's responsibility' if schools are not allowed to develop the necessary resources within their own management structures. Whereas Thomas concludes that local authority services should be devolved almost immediately to schools, Moore and Morrison (1988) argue for an 'interim' period of service, where the focus of support is the development of self-managing services within the schools. The difference in approach here is critical. The first appears to acquiesce to the notion of market forces, sink or swim, without clear safeguards or direction, whereas the second acknowledges a transitional role for the LEA, that of providing and guiding a strategy which will lead to local decision-making within the context of self-managing schools. Further, Thomas does not recognize the monitoring role of the LEA as defined by the Education Act 1988. It is of course both desirable and essential that the self-managing schools devise systems of self-review. In the meantime a strategic view of the local authority which leads schools towards accepting total responsibility for all pupils in or beyond the year 2000 must, I would suggest, contain the function of total quality control.

A local education authority strategy

What then will local authority strategy look like? First and foremost it will have a mechanism for funding needs both within the mainstream and within specialist provision which is not category based but which recognizes levels of support required by individual pupils. Preferably, this funding mechanism will not be affected by the 1981 Act assessment procedures, but will be consistent and continuous so as to encompass all aspects and degrees of need. Secondly, there will be a mechanism within each self-managing school which systematically reviews the identified needs of individual pupils to which the funding arrangements relate. Thirdly, as a consequence of this in-school review process there will be a need to moderate judgements made by schools much as there is a moderation of other teacher judgements on pupil performance such as examination work. This is likely to take the form of agreement trialling as is the case with the Standard Assessment Tasks. Fourthly, where levels of need are deemed by the in-school review to require a more concentrated support response, perhaps requiring focused expertise such as might be the case with a child experiencing severe communication difficulties, then the local authority could localize its support in the form of a local advisory/support structure servicing a defined community of schools.

In the longer term, one might envisage that the schools themselves would take over the funding and management of such a resource, through consortium arrangements, perhaps with each school taking a lead on a particular aspect of difficulty as described in the community response to special needs below. Finally, in the interim stage and possibly as a long-term role, the local authority will monitor the total needs requirement of a group of schools and broker support through the development of Service Level Agreements (SLA) with providers, such as peripatetic behavioural support, who will themselves be self-managing.

It follows from the above, that all of the local authority's services will, in time, be self-managing, and this includes special schools through the Local Management of Special Schools scheme (LMSS). The strategic and quality assurance roles described above should ensure that each group of schools has access to locally-managed services which they may buy singularly or in consortia. Critical to the success of such a strategy, however, will be the audit of need undertaken in the school.

A community response

Should there be any group of pupils for whom the self-managing school is unable to manage resources? For those opposed in principle to local management of schools there is a very real danger schools will not want to take this level of responsibility; but is partial acceptance admissible? Having embraced so enthusiastically the rights which go with local management ought not schools, and in particular their governors, also embrace the responsibilities inherent in this new found community role? Whether this will happen depends on two factors. Firstly, the attitude of governors towards the notion of service to the community as against customer satisfaction within a free market. Secondly, the removal of the option of a local authority mechanism which absorbs other people's problems. How the local authority of the present can plan strategically for this scenario is discussed below. The essential point here is the need to find ways and means of helping governors and teachers re-construct their view of special educational needs. Ultimately, governing bodies should be responsible for the commissioning of assessment and support and the monitoring of its effectivenss.

Whilst the majority of needs will be met through curriculum planning, some pupil needs will be of such an order as to require a clear decision on the part of the governing body, with the parent and pupil, to purchase special provision. If the 1981 Act is retained this function will most likely be carried out by the local authority but there is no reason to suppose that schools could not come together to provide most of the services that they need by retaining self-managing providers within their own consortia. How might this work? Schools would need to develop certain forms of complementary provision.

In the mid area of Kent, for example, this has already been achieved by the majority of secondary schools accepting responsibility for some aspect of severe and complex need. Within a radius of ten miles it is possible to visit secondary schools which take specific responsibility for integrating pupils with: severe learning difficulties, severe emotional and behavioural difficulties, moderate learning difficulties, language disorder, dyslexia, severe physical and medical disabilities. At the time of writing some of these schools intend to opt out; one is already a grant maintained school. This does not matter because the authority has a service level agreement with all of them and each knows what the other offers. The advantages are obvious; in a culture of competition it is possible to avoid special needs stigma through the sharing of responsibility. Other areas of Kent have similar agreements and of particular note is a City Technology College which has an integrated provision for pupils with hearing impairment and a facility for integrating pupils with severe learning difficulties from a nearby special school.

Where an authority has no strategy to move it in this direction, local management may intensify rejection. The Kent strategy is deliberately predicated on the notion that the local authority will have an interim role in developing such systems. That once its local advisory teams are in place and serviced by self-managing providers, whether they be mainstream integrated units, special schools or peripatetic services, the onus will be placed on all schools to respond positively and responsibly through the medium of the authority's audit of needs.

Implications for school management

One important mechanism for change which the local authority interim support structure can influence is the School Development Plan (SDP). As schools move steadily towards a more informed system of planning which takes account of resource allocation and staff training, it will be possible to introduce into this process mechanisms for heightening awareness of needs and clarifying in-school strategies. Through these mechanisms the deployment of resources to needs can be linked to a planning cycle of: an audit of needs, the development of achievable targets with realistic time-scales, the allocation of responsibilities, human and physical resource allocation, outcome evaluation.

The process by which schools arrive at an audit of need in respect of special educational needs, either for external funding or internal financial management, is a good example of how the local authority can influence this process. If it can offer nothing more than the proxy indicator of free school meals then it is missing a significant opportunity to shape attitudinal responses within schools. The Kent

Education Authority response to funding special educational needs, both within mainstream schools and within delegated units and locally managed special schools is a very good example of how the local authority can play a strategic role in the school development planning process.

Kent has developed a system of individual needs identification which removes the necessity for categorization and removes the demarcation between statemented and non-statemented pupils. Its five levels of support, based upon actual support requirements within the school, allows each school to quantify its resource needs. The nature of the descriptors used in the Special Educational Needs Audit, as it is called, allows governors and teachers to plan strategies to meet needs, thus encouraging further the concept of self-management. The levels of support are continuous and encompass at one end pupils who require a greater degree of curriculum differentiation, and at the other, pupils with profound and multiple disabilities. The audit is specifically designed to encourage schools to analyse and meet their own support needs. All five levels use the same analysis of need, which includes such aspects of classroom response as comprehension of task and collaborative working within a group. Teachers are asked to evaluate the level of support required by the pupil not in terms of disability but in terms of increasing amounts of: agency support, detail required for curriculum planning, direct support given by the teacher or classroom assistant and physical aids.

The audit is the cornerstone of Kent's strategy. It is only possible to devolve responsibility in full if there is a common understanding of what constitutes needs and response. The relative nature of special educational needs has consistently bedevilled local authority attempts to distribute resources equitably. Many authorities will testify to the lack of consistent assessment across both the same designation of need and different institutions providing for the same group of pupils. When Kent first ran its audit it found very wide discrepancies, both across geographical areas and across schools as to what constituted such traditional designations as learning difficulties, behavioural difficulties, and profound and multiple learning difficulties.

Interestingly all levels two to five in the National Curriculum could be found in special schools, just as levels one to four could be found in mainstream schools, with or without a statement. The moderation process has helped to address this imbalance of perception and Kent is now well placed to agree levels of need and response, and devolve resources equitably to self-managing institutions. Governors have taken a considerable interest in this process, with many special needs designated governors keeping a close eye on the audit process, its financial allocation and the manner in which the school disposes of its money. They are able to judge value for money by making a direct comparison between the audit action plan and resultant practice.

From the above it can be seen that the mainstream school of the future will require a considerably more sophisticated response to meeting special educational needs than is currently the case. An audit of need will be its most essential task. Of the remaining tasks the most important will be the introduction of a differentiated curriculum. Differentiation is a much used and ill-defined term but one nevertheless integral to a school's response to meeting all educational needs within the framework of self-management. The concept of individual difference is inseparable from it.

Moore (1992) has described the process of differentiation as planning classroom experiences at five distinct stages across three dimensions of school management. The stages are curriculum support, described by Moore as planned skill-sharing, units of work or the translation of National Curriculum Programmes of Study into a series of well-defined educational experiences, material adaptation within the classroom, groupings within the classroom and across the school, support for individuals and curriculum-based assessment. Moore has produced a matrix which identifies the needs of each stage at the management levels of the classroom teacher, key stage or department and whole school. The matrix identifies the critical relationships between whole school planning and classroom performance. In a self-managing environment each school will need to undertake this kind of analysis. Subsequent data will enable the senior management and governors of the school to make priority decisions in such crucial areas as staff deployment, classroom/department resources and staff development.

Such a movement would give credence to Moore and Morrison's assertion that current special educational needs support systems, both within local authorities and within schools, represent but an 'interim' stage in the more protracted development of resourced schools; defined by them as the interplay between staff *educated* in accommodating individual difference and appropriate material resources. If we substitute 'self-managed' for 'resourced', this would seem to be an accurate assessment. The interplay between suitably educated personnel and appropriate material resources is essentially what management within the self-managing school is about.

Conclusion

How will the self-managing school manage? If local authorities adopt an interim support role and provide a clear pathway to devolution through a well conceived strategy, and central government allow for appropriate levels of resource, the answer should be a positive one. Providing, of course, that school management, and that includes governors, can rise to the challenge of the school for all.

References

The Audit Commission for Local Authorities in England and Wales (1989) *Losing An Empire, Finding A Future: The LEA of the future.* London: H.M.S.O.

Coopers and Lybrand Deloitte (1992) *The Future Role Of Local Education Authorities.* London: Association of County Councils.

Moore, J. and Morrison, N (1988) *Someone Else's Problem? Teacher development to meet special educational needs.* London: Falmer Press.

Moore, J. (1991) Local Education Authority Re-structuring Under ERA: Meeting or creating special educational needs? *Support For Learning* 6 1.

Moore, J. (1992) 'Good planning is the key'. *British Journal of Special Education,* 19. 1. 16–19.

Sayer, J. (1987) *Secondary Schools For All? Strategies For Special Needs.* London: Cassell.

Thomas, G. (1992) 'Local authorities, special needs, and the status quo', *Support For Learning* 7 1.

CHAPTER 12

Raising Standards: Sticking to First Principles

Tony Booth

I am daunted by the title of this book. Together we are meant to rethink the way special needs can be met in mainstream schools. In his survey of mainstream special needs practice, Alan Dyson (1992) has distinguished between 'state of the art' good practice in schools and 'innovatory practice' which is at the cutting edge of new transformations of learning support and development. If I apply this distinction to my task I suspect that I am meant to put aside my ordinary 'state of the art' thoughts and try to be especially inventive. However, in this chapter, I will argue that it is important that we cling onto some of our old thoughts. I will consider those things that should stay the same as well as those that will or should alter.

I will suggest that the main function of the terms 'special needs' or 'special education' is to signal an enduring, common concern with students who experience difficulties or have disabilities in education. I will consider the conflicting principles that inform the approaches to diversity in our schools. I will ask whether our common concern with young people who experience difficulties and with disabled students leads us to adopt one set of principles rather than another. I will argue that there is often insufficient acknowledgement of the principles which inform everyday practice and that this can lead to contradictions which undermine the intentions of educators. In particular, I will discuss some of the problems with the widely used language of special needs. While our concerns with vulnerable students, and our principles and the critique of practice which follow from them, may remain unchanged, I will discuss how the circumstances of education and the particular vulnerabilities which demand our attention, alter.

I am almost at the end of writing for a course 'Learning for all', that, with minor modification, is meant to last until 1999. Because of this time scale, we have to search for perennial questions and enduring principles that will stay relevant as the world of education changes. Schools contain children and young people that differ in backgrounds, attainments and interests. How should they respond to the diversity of their students? How can difficulties in learning and disaffection be prevented or reduced? What principles can guide the practice of teachers and other school workers in meeting these challenges?

What stays the same?

Our common concern with students who experience difficulties in schools or who have disabilities is very broad. As well as students who experience difficulties in learning there are disaffected and distressed students. Of disabled students, only some experience difficulties in learning or are disaffected or distressed.

We share an interest in reducing the difficulties students encounter but are we also committed to a common set of principles to inform our practice? The notions of 'good practice' or 'state of the art practice' or 'innovatory practice' presume a common purpose. Yet what is good or innovatory for some, may be anathema to others. At the time of writing, Goebbels' diaries are being serialized in the *Sunday Times*. The innovatory solution to diversity associated with Goebbels is not part of what most of us would regard as good practice. What other practices does our common concern exclude?

There are two opposing solutions to teaching a diversity of students in schools which can be called 'selective' and 'inclusive'. Each is informed by a set of moral and political values which in turn limit the approaches to reducing difficulties in schools, to raising standards. The selective approach starts from the assumption that learning takes place best in groups of 'similar' learners and involves a search for ways of selecting and matching students, methods, curricula and schools. It assumes further that the process and prospect of selection provide incentives to try harder and disincentives to falling behind. One teacher encountered a blatant example of such a view when he went for a job interview to teach environmental science and discovered that his own subject was near the bottom of the status hierarchy:

> The curriculum was described as 'normal science for the able pupils, general science for the less able, environmental studies for

the still weaker pupils and horticulture for the really low ability'. I described this as an attitude of 'vegetables for the vegetables' and did not get the job. (Fairhurst, 1992)

The inclusive approach begins by accepting and valuing the heterogeneous nature of learning groups and seeks teaching methods, curricula, and ways of organizing resources to support and increase this diversity. On this view a shared experience in mixed groups can form the basis for differentiated teaching and learning. Bernard Fairhurst described his approach to involving his class group and the community of the school in the development of a mixed-habitat area at his school in Gloucestershire.

Initial stages involved showing students the bit of school field, identifying the range of plants present and discussing how variety could be increased. Then drawing scale plans with the pupils designing a mixed-habitat area with all possible inclusions coming from them, for example, pond, marsh, grassland, shrubs. As well as looking at the area, I prompted them with questions, e.g. 'How would you encourage amphibians?... reptiles?... flying mammals?... hedgehogs?... butterflies?' These provoked further thoughts and additions to plans. The questions 'What about access for people in wheelchairs? Or plants for people who are visually impaired?' provoked various responses from interest and appreciating the need to rethink access, pathways, height of beds, varieties etc., to 'What has that got to do with a habitat area' or 'What has that got to do with our school?' We discussed the role of our school in providing a service to all the community.

Environmental science, besides providing an infinite variety of fruitful shared experiences for students, is also a fertile source of metaphors for education and society. However, the metaphors that you choose depend on your ideological preconceptions. Competition for ecological niches and a struggle for survival may seem suitable models for a selective classroom environment. Alternatively the creation of a mixed habitat in which a diversity of plants and animals flourish and which may require careful, planned and repeated intervention may be seen as a model of inclusive education.

I have argued that an inclusive approach to education can be informed by three related principles. A *comprehensive principle* is concerned with educating the diversity of students in a community, together, in nursery, primary and secondary schools. An *integration principle* is concerned with the process of increasing the partici-pation of children and young people who experience difficulties in learning or have disabilities within the mainstream of education. *A principle of equality of value* is concerned with the reduction of discrimination against children and young people in education on the basis of their gender, class, race, family structure, culture, sexual orientation, disabilities or attainments.

The first two of these have obvious counter principles, of *selection* and *segregation.* I would argue that selection and segregation are inevitably bound up with the ascription of differences in value to students on the basis of background, attainment and disability. The devaluation of students creates a pool of potential disaffection which contributes to difficulties in learning. In contributing to devaluation and difficulties in learning a selective approach to diversity conflicts with our common concern. For this reason the selective solution to raising standards is ultimately self-defeating.

Of course the same slogan can be used to underpin widely different practices. A *democratic principle* might be seen to incor-porate other inclusive principles with their emphasis on community participation. However in the last decade in the guise of a '*principle for choice*' it has been used to promote selection. Equally I stress an approach to integration which is about 'education for diversity' whereas others have fitted a selective philosophy onto their view of integration either by introducing a cut-off by 'presumed ability' for those students with disabilities who are acceptable within the mainstream or by promoting a narrow view of normalization. The latter is most marked in those who advocate the inclusion of deaf students in the mainstream through the promotion of oral-only methods of communication. (Lynas, 1986)

Applying principles in practice

Practice itself is often informed by conflicting principles which push in opposing directions. For example, rigid setting arrangements may be created alongside an attempt to value the diversity of backgrounds of students. I am currently exploring the nature of, and conflicts between, categorization procedures in those compre-hensive schools which include students categorized as having severe learning difficulties. However, that different practices depend on different principles seems to come as a surprise to some people.

Trevor Payne (1991) has questioned the preoccupation with in-class, rather than withdrawal, support in the following way:

> With very few exceptions, readers and audiences were exhorted to embrace the concept of in-class support for children with learning difficulties as a *fait accompli*, as an almost moral and social imperative. Those teachers still daring to actually withdraw children from their mainstream classes for 'remedial tuition' (both unfashionable words) must have felt like accomplices to some form of educational apartheid.

I think Trevor Payne is right in drawing attention to a real problem, like others before him (e.g. Matthews, 1987). Some teachers do avoid withdrawal because they think it is frowned upon. But he misunderstands the source of the difficulty. It arises because, usually, the relationship between principles and practices are left unstated. In-class support is promoted, at least in part, because when used effectively it can help to promote inclusive classroom strategies for differentiating curricula. Withdrawal is rejected as a general solution to resolving difficulties in learning because it helps to support the myth of homogeneity: that most students require the same approach and content in their lessons, which in turn promotes inflexible teaching. This does not mean that withdrawal is an evil, but an ordinary part of students education, no more remarkable than a music lesson.

The language of special needs

The language, or jargon, of special needs is also part of a selective philosophy and I believe that it stands in the way of the development of teaching and supporting diverse groups in our schools. If I did not have theoretical objections to the way it perpetuates perceived divisions between 'normal' and 'abnormal' learners my experience tells me that it provides ineffective communication in practice. Writers often sense this and reveal how the notion of special needs prevents a rethinking of the way students are categorized, when they try to explain themselves. In a book called *Humanities for All*, in a series on *Special Needs in the Ordinary School*, Clarke and Wrigley (1988) tell us that 'Our chief interest is with those who, under a different classification used to be called slow learners.' And what should we make of the remark of our mentors in the soon-to-be-privatized HMI, that 'Nationally, pupils whose *disabilities* are such that they have special needs at some time in their schooling constitute about 20 per cent of the school population?' (DES 1991, my emphasis). If such a remark tells me anything, it is that I'd better hold onto my old thoughts for a while longer.

Phrases like 'children with special needs' or 'students with learning difficulties' encourage a view of school problems as originating within the deficiencies of students. This is a well known and apparently widely accepted argument yet it is rarely implemented. One of the barriers to changing the way we speak and write is that we are forced into using the silly definitions of the 1981 Act in the statementing process. You will remember that the act tells us that all students in wheelchairs have learning difficulties and that the absence of English as a first language does not contribute to difficulties in learning in our schools. But if you have any doubts about the cumbersome nature of the language, find a copy of the 1981 Act and try expressing which students with learning difficulties should be the subject of statements. You will discover that these are 'pupils who have learning difficulties which call for special educational provision to be made for them ... which calls for the authority to determine the special provision that should be made for them'.

The sensible option, outside of the statementing process, is to take control of the way we use language. I have suggested that we talk of students who *experience difficulties in learning* in schools to reflect the way such difficulties arise in a relationship between teachers, students and curricula. This language matches the work that many 'learning support' or 'learning development' teachers do in encouraging appropriate curricula for all students. It also defines a role that is as applicable to supporting teachers working within a group of students with very limited speech and comprehension of language as to students struggling in a GCSE class. Robert Hull (1985) has recorded the language gap and gulf in understanding between many students and teachers across and up and down the curriculum and I draw on his work whenever I need to remind myself of such issues.

We are told, frequently, that standards have fallen in education. The way 'needs' in education are discussed may be a pertinent example. Every newspaper I open carries an advertisement for school inspectors from the newly named Department For Education telling me that schools need testing just as much as children. I have argued, for a long time, that there was something wrong with the language of educational needs. It portrayed needs in education as transparently in the interests of children and young people as if they were simple bodily requirements like food. It permitted otherwise talented educationalists to maintain that educational conflicts, like that surrounding the notion of integration, could be resolved according to the needs of students; that lurking within each student was a marker awaiting detection, indicating whether his or her education should take place amongst or separate from the mainstream. 'At a time when it is regarded as good professional practice to identify the specific needs of each individual child, is it not possible,' asked Peter Mittler in 1985, 'that the needs of at least some children are better met in a particular special school?' Integration would, on this view, spring into being if, on the basis of professional assessments, students were found to need it. The argument can be used to obscure the process whereby the 'needs' of students are made to fit with existing provision.

I had felt that 'needs in education' might often conform to another meaning of need, when we talk of someone as 'needing a good talking to', or a child as 'needing a good hiding'. But at least the ambiguity was there, even if it did confuse many teachers, educational psychologists and others. Many did strive valiantly to turn the language of need to the advantage of students and their families; to understand and try to act in their interests. Now, however the message from Central Government seems to be clear. Schools and children need to be kept in line. The line they 'need' to be kept in has streams and sets, desirable and undesirable schools. They 'need' selection.

If there is so much wrong with the language of 'special needs' why do we retain it? Does it serve the interests of special needs professionals, in defining a territory and status, rather than the interests of students in schools?

What changes?

It is clear that the circumstance in which principles are applied change dramatically. Central and local government policies and the level of resources create a kaleidoscope of shifting contexts. Priorities about which difficulties should receive our attention change, too. New priorities may be a product of changing policies or may force themselves on us through media and other social pressures. As priorities change it is inevitable that the work of those in the system who concern themselves with difficulties in schools will also change. There is a growing concern about those children, as yet small in number in the UK, who are infected with HIV or are affected by having a family member with HIV or AIDS. This is likely to form a greater preoccupation in the future. In the 1980s and early 1990s the miseries caused by child abuse, particularly child sexual abuse have received consistent recognition and publicity, including a number of cases where children have been abused while in the care of a local authority (see Booth *et al* 1992, Booth 1992). Since the late 1980s there has been a growing awareness of bullying amongst school children and a gradual recognition of racial and sexual harassment and sexist abuse as forms of bullying (see Skinner, 1992). The joint consideration of these issues may make it easier for teachers and others to understand the effects of each, and to see bullying as having its origins in the adult world rather in an, as yet, unsocialized childhood.

The pressures from the publication of school examination results, coupled with the new freedoms given to schools under local management has been blamed for the widespread and dramatic rise in exclusions from schools. A survey conducted by the National Union of Teachers in English and Welsh local authorities suggested that permanent and temporary exclusions affected 25,000 students a year and had risen by 20% in the previous year (NUT, 1992). The increases reported for some local education authorities were even more dramatic. As Stephen Byers, Chair of the Education Committee of the Association of Metropolitan Authorities reported:

> It's a national problem. It's happening throughout the country. In Newcastle there's been something like a 50% increase from one year to the next ... What's particularly worrying is the number of exclusions in the primary sector. You wouldn't have thought that those pupils aged 5–11 would be subject to exclusions. To go back to Newcastle again, there's been 30% increase in primary school exclusions from one year to the next, the same in Leeds; a big increase in primary school exclusions. It's a trend that should give all of us concern. (You and Yours, 29th January 1992)

There is clear further evidence that the growth in exclusions is disproportionately affecting students of Afro-Caribbean origin (Nottingham County Council 1991, London Borough of Lewisham

1991). This exacerbates a long standing problem and David Gillborn has conducted a careful study of the way students of Afro-Caribbean origin can be treated negatively and subject to stereotyped attitudes and intolerance of their differences of culture (Gillborn 1990). If there is decreasing tolerance of difference in some schools this may explain the rise in exclusion rates and must be a concern of all those who wish to reduce the difficulties students face in schools. Could our common concern be extended so that it encompasses all students who are devalued within schools or insufficiently included within the curricula and social life of the mainstream?

Change which should have taken place in some areas of practice has been limited. The rigid demarcation which still exists in some schools, between those who are meant to respond to difficulties of behaviour and control and those who busy themselves with supporting learning makes little theoretical or practical sense. The major impact teachers can make in reducing disaffection in schools is through the curriculum just as it is for preventing and reducing difficulties in learning.

We have still a long way to go, too, before there is an acceptance of diversity in the sexual orientation of students. About 10% of young people grow up as gay or lesbian. They often feel a sense of exclusion which may interfere with learning in school. Now I think that we should accept and value the diversity of students as a good in itself, not because it may raise attainment levels. But pointing to the difficulties that devaluation of some students may cause in terms of creating disaffection and underachievement multiplies the reasons why this becomes a central concern of those who profess an interest in reducing school difficulties in general and difficulties in learning in particular.

Concluding remark

In this chapter I have revisited some old thoughts about the relationship between principles and the reduction of exclusionary pressures and practices in schools and classrooms. I think it is important to keep hold of a clear set of principles that inform our approach to diversity in schools, and to make them explicit, even if this leads to conflict. That education changes through consensus is a false belief that enables those with power to reduce opposition to their policies. Changes in education which started

140

with the so-called discussion papers issued at the beginning of the summer break in 1987, which preceded the autumn 1987 Education Bill which presaged the 1988 Education Act, can be likened to a Thurber cartoon which has struck in my mind since childhood. It depicts two fencers. One of them cries '*touché*' as he swings and cuts off the head of the other. There is a look of affront and recrimination in the eyes of the severed head at this breach of etiquette. But it is too late.

However, I think there are several reasons for thinking that the moves towards more selective and competitive schools may falter. I have mentioned the problem of exclusions, which may be pointing up a politically unacceptable end result of selective politices within schools. But the main cause for optimism is that parents do not want their local schools to become extinct in the struggle for survival. Most parents want a good local school. A good local school is one that serves and values all the members of its community.

References

Booth, T., Swann, W., Potts, P. and Masterton, M., Ed., (1992) *Learning for All: Curricula for diversity in education*. London: Routledge.

Booth, T. (1992) 'Making connections', Unit 1/2 of E242 *Learning for All*. Milton Keynes: Open University.

Clarke, J., and Wrigley, K. (1988) *Humanities for All*. London: Cassell.

Department of Education and Science (1991) *Special Needs and the National Curriculum: a report by HM Inspectorate*. London: HMSO.

Dyson, A. (1992) 'Innovatory mainstream practice. What's happening in schools' provision for special needs?', *Support for Learning*, 7, 2, 51–87.

Fairhurst, B. (1992) Personal communication.

Gillborn, D. (1990) *Race, Ethnicity and Education*. London: Unwin-Hyman.

Hull, R. (1985) *The Language Gap*. London: Methuen.

Lynas, W. (1986) *Integrating the Handicapped into Ordinary Schools, a Study of Hearing Impaired Pupils*. London: Croom Helm.

London Borough of Lewisham (1991) *Pupil Exclusions From Schools*. London: London Borough of Lewisham.

Mathews, H. (1987) 'The place of withdrawal', in Booth, T., Potts, P., Swann, W., (ed.), *Preventing Difficulties in Learning*. Oxford: Blackwell.

Mittler, P. (1985) 'Integration, the shadow and the substance', *Education and Child Psychology*, 2, 3, 8–22.

National Union of Teachers (1992) *Union Survey Reveals Jump in Pupils' Exclusions*. London: NUT.

Nottinghamshire County Council (1991) *Pupils' Exclusions from Nottingham Secondary Schools*. Nottingham: Nottingham County Council.

Payne, T. (1991) 'It's cold in the other room', *Support for Learning*, 6, 2, 61–5.

Skinner, A. (1992) *Bullying: An annotated bibliography of literature and resources*. Leicester: Youth Work Press.

CHAPTER 13

Effective Thinking or Effective Policy?

Roy Evans

> The great difficulty in education is to get experience out of idea.
> (George Santayana *The Life of Reason*.)

> The greater part of our lives is spent in dreaming over the morrow, and when it comes, it, too, is consumed in the anticipation of a brighter morrow, and so the cheat is prolonged, even to the grave. (Mark Rutherford *The Deliverance*.)

It appears to have become increasingly commonplace for educators to be tempted, through the provenance of hindsight, towards a degree of historical revisionism when considering the principles upon which significant reforms in policy and practice have been built. Observable, assessable features of current organization and practice are viewed as operational outcomes of 'policy'. A simplistic notion of cause and effect seems to have invaded reason to the point where the legitimacy, coherency, cogency and defensibility of the intellectual scaffolding to legislative change are judged in terms of the utility of emergent systems and sub-systems at local authority and school level. The hindsight tendency seems to suggest that if the systems that have been created and the procedures that have been established prove inadequate, for example, to meet the special educational needs of each child, then the principles on which they were established are perhaps in need of revision. At local level this is possibly true ... given that there are a plethora of reasons why systems may fail; one may understand such a short step whilst disagreeing with the diagnosis. What is less tenable is to take the larger step and propose that system inadequacy at the point of delivery is historically rooted in the conceptual inappropriateness of the guiding legislation. The temptation to take such a step does appear to have been too strong for some to resist.

Within the present book reconceptualization is a central theme. It may appear to be more than amply justified in the light of the report of the Audit Commission during late June (1992) on the current state of provision for children with special needs. Commenting on the long delays in reaching a final statement, on the unhelpful and opaque manner in which many statements were written and the degree to which proposed provision was manifestly resources driven, the report argues powerfully for urgent revisions which will more effectively serve the legal rights of children and their parents. The Commission's Report follows in the wake of much recent concern over increasing numbers of children being excluded from school and denied proper access to the National Curriculum. Such concern reflects not only the experience of teachers and educators in various contexts (see Evans and Lovey 1992), but has achieved wide coverage in the media. More than a year ago the Centre for the Study of Integration in Education (CSIE) (1991) drew attention to the 'disturbing increases in the segregation of children in special schools in some parts of the country'. Of particular concern to CSIE was the level of exportation of children with special needs not only out of Borough but also out of the state sector into independent special schools. The CSIE report aptly comments that this trend 'makes a mockery of each child's fundamental right to belong to their local ordinary school'.

Whilst the trend of the past eighteen months is understandable, and was probably the predictable outcome of Local Management of Schools (LMS) in so far as ordinary schools are concerned, the basic obstacles to the implementation of the 1981 Act in the spirit of the Warnock Report (1987) arose, I would suggest, for other reasons. One of these reasons is startlingly evident in the title of the Audit Commission's report, *Getting in on the Act: provision for pupils with special educational needs,* which then unashamedly addresses the plight of the traditional 2%. Whatever the term was meant to invoke from a conceptual standpoint, its use in every day situations and contexts subsequently defines its operational meaning. The only surprising feature of the Audit Commission's report is that it has taken Government, through its inspectorial watchdog, quite so long to actually say what many teachers have known since the mid-eighties. In short, the Act has been hijacked by the local education authorities. The search for neat administrative solutions to complex human problems has the effect of redesignating and redefining what constitutes a difficulty which carries a resource implication. Whilst patterns vary nationally, the overall tendency following April 1983 was to expand local authorities' capacity for responding to perceived legal obligations and to emphasize procedural knowledge relating to statements. Apart from the deleterious effect this had on the capability of educational psychologists to offer advice to teachers on a range of educational psychological difficulties it also sent a clear message to teachers concerning what 'special' *really* meant.

Emergent meanings

As long ago as 1986, Campbell pointed up the almost complete lack of utility of the Statements of Special Educational Needs within an Inner London Borough. He observed that there were a number of reasons for this. One of these reasons has its reflection in the Audit Commission's own report. Generally, statements can be of little or no value to teachers in operationalizing the curriculum plan for the child because they have not been perceived as curriculum documents. Campbell noted the unhelpful nature of statements which more or less said (and some cases actually did say) 'provision to meet the above'. Although not without its own difficulties, the requirements of the Individual Education Programme (IEP) in the USA, created within the regulations of Public Law 94–142, are far more consistent with teachers' needs for positive helpful advice and direction. It is also worth noting that throughout the eighties, Her Majesty's Inspectors' (HMI) position in relation to special needs was to the effect that these terms made sense only when expressed in curriculum terms. The National Curriculum's Task Group under Ron Davie's chairmanship went to considerable lengths to emphasize the curricular and pedagogic character of 'entitlement'. Significantly however, the wisdom contained within *Curriculum Guidance 2* will have little impact on teachers' practice until they own a conception of special educational needs which is consistent with the driving ideology of the 1981 Act. For many teachers still, this will require a re-examination of their implicit theories of attribution in respect of 'learning difficulties'. This is an important issue which will be returned to. In the absence of a clear conception of 'specialness', the recent publication by the National Curriculum Council of *Curriculum Guidance 9 and 10* will hardly impact on teachers' practice.

Some further points raised by Campbell (1986) are worth making here. Given the potential opacity of statements, it has been the experience of many schools and headteachers that little opportunity has existed for an interpretive consultation with external agents in regard to the translation into practice of key features of statemented provision. Not uncommonly there are related issues connected with the provision of identified support for an individual child for a proportion of the teaching week. Some of these issues relate directly to the rigidity with which 'in-class' support teaching is contractually written by the local authority with no consultation with the head of the receiving school or with the relevant class teacher. The Individual Support Teacher (IST) is a phenomenon of the eighties. Contracted to work with one child, the support teacher is an administrator's solution to meeting the legal requirements of a statement for a child placed in the ordinary school.

Our own work has led us to review the attitudes of class teachers to the support teacher alongside other forms of in-class support that have burgeoned in the wake of post-Warnock rhetoric. The survey by Evans, Fry, Neville-Jones and Cawley (1992) of a sample of schools in one London borough reveal that conceptions of support roles are still heavily conflicted in respect of shared working, joint planning, curriculum differentiation and task setting. The survey also reveals that in respect of the more generic form of SEN support available in some schools the issues raised by Hart in the mid-eighties have not only not been addressed but are still, for a good many teachers, unrecognized questions. Of particular concern is the evidence to the effect that of teachers surveyed, including heads, deputies, special needs co-ordinators, special needs support teachers and class teachers, fewer than 10% claimed any formal expertise through qualification or through attendance on a substantial in-service course. The latter we subsequently identified as something akin to a one term in-service (OTIS) course or relevant modules within an in-service BEd/Diploma or Modular Master's programme. Amongst support teachers in the sample the level of expertise claimed was actually lower than in the sample as a whole. In fact, many were part-time, short-contract teacher returners. We have no reason to believe that this particular local authority is atypical of Outer London Boroughs and would suggest that in significant respects it is better than most. It has not suffered historically the problems of retention and supply in respect of qualified teachers that has characterized provision in many Inner London authorities.

Nevertheless, conceptions of support for non-statemented children with special needs in ordinary schools is little different from two or three decades ago. Except in one significant respect: concern for children with difficulties with basic skills and behaviour is now rehearsed, not through a contextually focused paradigm of instruction, *but* through a model of resource utilization heavily influenced by the rhetoric of equity and largely unaccountable in terms of evidence of efficacy. In this latter regard also it is reminiscent of the fate of 'remedial' services. Although Hanko's modelling of shared expertise and joint problem solving has enjoyed some success, it is potentially open to the same criticism as Schön's Reflective Practitioner: at the end of the day, teachers must be able to reflect on something: there must be a recognizable expertise that is worth sharing. It may be appropriate, and given the theme of this book, even timely, to consider whether the tides and currents encountered during the voyage of re-discovery, which has been the educational experience for a decade, have brought us to the New World. Or whether we have unknowingly passed it by and come full circle to where we used to be?

A major strand within the literature concerning children with special needs in the ordinary school has been concerned with the demystification of practices traditionally attributed to peripatetic remedial teachers and special needs support teams. Frequently in the past decade, in the professional literature, at regional and national conferences the call has been to enskill class teachers, to share knowledge and expertise, to ensure ownership of special needs issues by enabling ordinary teachers to acquire enlarged repertoires of pedagogic strategies. All this, through working with a special needs teacher who possessed shareable knowledge and skills. The oft repeated phrase 'the teacher is the key' entered the language of trainers and became the pivotal concept for training (in Essex for instance, an entire training package was built around it). The clear presumption is that there exists a body of consultative knowledge that can be accessed and can be made accessible to teachers. To a point this is workable provided:

- advisory support teams exist and can in principle be deployed on demand. They may carry one of a variety of names as Gipps, Gross and Goldstein (1987) point out. It is important however that they exist
- individual advisory teachers or advisers/inspectors have received an appropriate training. Appropriate, that is, to the support that they are likely to be called upon to deliver. This is partly about professional credibility and partly about resourcing the model of teacher development that creates their operational role. There is a presumption that such teachers have an expertise connected with learning disabilities and a disposition to share that expertise with others.

At this point in time two questions may be asked of future arrangements. Firstly, as advisory teams disappear and/or their services increasingly commodified and marketed, who resources the model of practice erected by 'the teacher is the key'?

Secondly, who defines professional expertise? If there is a special knowledge connected with leadership roles in respect of special educational needs, is there a broad consensus on how it may be described? Are there desirable experiences, skills, attitudes and competence that those in pivotal positions in schools and local authorities should possess? If we are to remain seriously committed to the notions of equity espoused by Warnock, should not *all* special needs co-ordinators in all schools be minimally certificated in terms that will support the range of curricular responses that colleagues may be called upon to make? Patterns may vary, but very many special needs co-ordinators in primary schools received little or no training prior to taking up the role. The one-term in-service courses were an excellent introduction but the declining resource base in support of local policy initiatives has effectively limited provision in this sense. Growth of modular course structures has provided opportunity for local authorities and schools to buy into specialist courses either on an auditing or Credit Accumulation and Transfer (CAT) basis and build qualifications over four years or more. Responding flexibly to consumer choice does, however, raise issues connected with the sequencing of courses and puts coherency at risk. The need for training was identified by the Warnock Committee as a priority. I believe it remains so despite the money available through Grant Related In-Service Training (GRIST) and LEA Training Grant Schemes (LEATGS) and the Council for the Accreditation of Teacher Education (CATE) requirements in respect of initial training.

Alongside the rehearsed rhetoric of 'demystification' and 'teacher is the key' there has been an associated effort directed sharply at what may crudely be called teachers' implicit theories of attribution in respect of special needs. We seem to have understood that reference to external features of a child's experience, external to school that is, was not particularly helpful when these became erected as reasons for poor in-school response. We seem also to be committed professionally to the view that whilst learning difficulties were, in essence, social constructs, the classroom was where learning was intentionally constructed. This is not to deny the social ecological view but rather to emphasise the power of the teacher in influencing educational outcomes. Attributing learning failure to faulty pedagogy, poor classroom organization, inadequate task design or generally poor attitudes on the part of the teacher has not always been accepted and not always understood. There is also an argument in support of the view that such a model of attribution is in any case a crass oversimplification of the nature of human experience. That apart, there has been an argument that to focus teachers' thinking on ways of diagnosing difficulties, removing hindrances to learning and attending to the character of the tasks set is in any case what good teaching is all about. The individualized teaching approach emphasizes what the teacher can do and acts as countermeasure to the essential defeatism associated with undue appeal to external unmodifiable factors. At this point we experience further difficulties.

Conway's (1989) study of teacher attitudes to special educational needs in an outer London borough revealed that within her sample the over-riding tendency was to seek explanation of children's difficulties by appeal to precisely those factors to which I have referred as essentially non-modifiable. Conway's study was, to a degree, influenced by the Croll and Moses work (1985) conducted a number of years earlier and which sought to elicit explanations of learning and behaviour problems from amongst over 400 junior school heads and teachers. The

Croll and Moses study was interesting in so far as it refers to a period not long removed from the implementation of the Education Act at which time their study suggested that relatively few explanations invoked school characteristics as causally relevant. Around two thirds of their reported explanations for poor discipline and emotional/behavioural difficulties were directed to external-to-school factors. Conway's study five years later focused upon an analysis of end-of-year reports on children in five Inner-London junior schools who had been referred to educational psychologists because of their learning difficulties. Her analyses of the written reports reveal that teachers referred to a range of personal qualities in the child to explain learning difficulties. Conway posits four as particularly powerful. These were:

- Poor intellectual ability
  Nathalie is full of enthusiasm and self motivation in practical and creative activities, but is not academically oriented

- Lack of will power
  Darren finds it very difficult to produce a complete piece of written work even after days of repeated urging

- Poor motivation
  Because of work avoidance tactics in mathematics and other areas he has not covered as much work as he would have were he better motivated

- Lack of self-restraint
  He encourages himself to give way to aggressive tendencies when in conflict with other children. . . .

Following in-depth interviews with the teachers concerned, Conway (1989) observes that no teacher formulated her comments in terms of her own practice although all were prompted to consider factors within the school. More recently, Evans and Shaw's (1991) in-depth case study of one large Inner-London primary school revealed a similar disposition to avoid focusing on classroom practice in explaining learning and behavioural difficulties. The poverty of the area, one-parenthood, small overcrowded flats in high rise blocks all figured in teachers' attribution of the causes of indiscipline:

- 'What can you expect? They have nowhere to play, so they come to school and let off steam.' (Deputy head teacher)
- 'College didn't really prepare me for this. It was a good course like, but tutors didn't really have enough time to deal with all the sorts of difficulties that children can have.' (Probationer)
- 'I think we could be of more help to the teachers if we could get to know a few children much better. But nobody asks us what we think and we are not invited to staff meetings.' (Ancillary helper)
- 'Most of them are not bad kids. I know many of their parents 'cos I live in the area. Most of them wouldn't dare behave at home like they behave here. They need firm handling or they'll take advantage. It's only natural, innit?' (School secretary)

The professional reality defined by the totality of such views suggests that this school has much to discuss as it seeks to evolve an effective whole school approach to special needs. There are ideological as well as strategic issues at stake. The conceptualization of the problem will evidently affect the means sought to its solution. Many schools remain in this position. Despite a decade of advice and guidance, unprecedented sums of money made available for professional development, the highlighting of special needs issues at national and local level, the legal obligation placed on schools to identify and meet all cases of learning difficulty wherever and however they arise, some of the fundamental keys to the improvement of practice are still not owned by teachers. **Would a reconceptualization of special educational needs help? I suspect that the answer to this question is probably no!** There are several reasons to suggest this.

Firstly, there is no reason to suppose that the current tendency to confuse the organization of provision with the organization of learning would be any less evident in a new conceptualization. Meeting children's special educational needs is only peripherally to do with how resources are deployed. It is centrally connected to the use made of the resources that are available. Elegant structures for deploying and utilizing human resources are, at the end of the day, quite valueless if individual children experience no net benefit.

Secondly, although special needs issues must be compulsorily dealt with in the scope of initial training one cannot be sanguine that students will necessarily emerge into their first post with an appropriate understanding of key concepts. It will depend in no small measure on how the training institution organizes its work in relation to special needs. Current wisdom favours the permeation of special needs issues throughout curriculum and teaching studies. Whilst the central purpose here is to achieve curriculum penetration, the model suffers from the obvious weakness that not all curriculum studies tutors are versed in the philosophy of Warnock or necessarily have the time or opportunity to develop with students appropriate strategies of differentiation within programmes of study. Whilst subject oriented tutors are expert in their own field, to whom do students turn for expert guidance in respect of specific learning difficulties, emotional and behavioural difficulties and strategies of intervention?

Thirdly, in the decade that has passed since the implementation of the 1981 Education Act, the capacity of the educational system to respond to the key tenets of the Act has been attenuated in consequence of numerous competing innovations. Some innovations are proving to generate operational outcomes that are diametrically opposite to those sought by the Act. The current effect of local management on school exclusion rates is just one example of how the 'principle' of inclusivity is being eroded through the increasing commodification of education and the perceived need to sell an image of schools which is achievement driven. Achievement, that is, in its raw sense, rather than its value added sense. The market place philosophy which schools are embracing contrasts starkly with the egalitarian ideals which underpinned the deliberations of the Warnock Committee. Informed by a growing international literature on educational intervention, what is nevertheless of signal importance within the Warnock recommendations is the sense of social justice conveyed. To this end the interconnectedness of many social institutions was emphasized. Systems Theory (Minuchin 19874, Bronfenbrenner 1979) has tended to see any given social institution, for example, the school or the family, as nested within a number of other societal systems. The actions of an individual, whether child, teacher or parent are influenced by and influence his context in constantly recurring sequences of interactions. Whilst the individual may be approached as a subsystem or part of the system, the whole must be taken into account. Changes within the macrosystem of society via, for example, the health of the national economy, create exogenous forces which ultimately exert influence at the level of the individual child. A substantial change of social policy at national level or a significant shift in the prevailing political *zeitgeist* will carry consequences for subsystems down to the level of the individual in school or in the family and will influence the character of interactions with the close meso-system of family, school and locality. Bronfenbrenner's social ecological view, that to change behaviour one needs to change environments, including the social psychological, also works in reverse. The problem that we face in respect of delivering on the conceptions of special educational need encapsulated within the 1981 Act needs to be viewed against the seismic shift in social and political values that occurred during the Thatcher years. These cannot be ignored because they manifest as political statements which carry the power to determine the legitimacy or otherwise of proposed interventions. In so doing they provide alternative explanations to human behaviour.

Conviction politics leads to the position that Lord Scarman was wrong, the Archbishop of Canterbury misguided and that poverty is neither cyclical (Joseph, 1985) nor an underlying factor in lawlessness, educational failure or underachievement. Conviction politics has taken the country to the point where the jobless are indolent and those who fall foul of the law are inherently sinful. This is problematic for educators at the point of designing innovation or implementing actions to support the basic provisions of the 1981 Act in the spirit of the Warnock Report. It is also problematic in so far as educational underachievement has become increasingly viewed as the essential outcome of non-effective schools and, more pointedly, poor or ineffective teaching. That children's educational achievement is influenced by the quality of teaching received is not at issue. Burt's seminal work (1937) recognized the point and countless generations of parents have known the strong and weak teachers in local schools. What is clearly absurd is that one social institution, the school, amongst the many by which children increasingly are influenced, is now seen to bear the entire burden of responsibility for children's poor response, low motivation, indiscipline, truanting, and, ultimately, alienation. The point made by Wedge and Prosser (1973) and Evans (1976), that educational underachievement was a complex phenomenon requiring multifaceted solutions involving a range of social institutions became increasingly unfashionable during the eighties and appears now to have become recast as a problem for pedagogics and curriculum delivery systems. Bernstein's oft quoted view that 'schools cannot compensate for society' (1970) is, of course, equally unfashionable.

Perhaps because of the value shift of the last decade and the massive burden of innovation that the system has been required to respond to, we appear, within the bounds of special educational needs provision, to have lost touch with our roots. That we have lost the initiative in reforming practice is beyond question. What then could we regard as our roots and, if we have been cut off from them, why has this happened?

Warnock ... patrimony and legacy

T.S. Eliot once observed *(Notes Towards the Definition of Culture)* that it was an abiding ambition to rescue the word 'culture'. Thinking about the disparate ways in which 'special needs' as a term has come to be employed leads one to understand perhaps that a similar rescue operation may be appropriate ... even if such attempt is fraught with difficulty. One over-riding difficulty is represented by Foucault's (1977) observation that it is impossible to achieve objectivity in analysing what appears to be, since the observer is inextricably part of the processes he attempts to analyse:

> A doctor can stand outside a patient and treat him objectively but a practitioner of interpretive analysis has no such external position. The disease he seeks to cure is a part of an epidemic which also affects him.

Edelman (1977) reiterates this position by denying the possibility of one objective reality, since the meaning and logic of any interpretation are located in the same frame of reference as the object of interpretation itself.

Treating both the Warnock Report and the 1981 Act as texts raises further difficulties. In the former case the report has historical interest for many thousands of young teachers who have entered the profession in the past fifteen years, including those for whom training carried mandatory treatment of special educational needs under the Council for Accreditation of Teacher Education (CATE) criteria. Even assuming that many will have interrogated the report at first hand, the interpretation gained of what Warnock 'meant' is by no means predictable. The change in social philosophy remarked on earlier will effect interpretation: of more substantial significance however is the extent to which many of the report's central principles are themselves social constructions, mediated by language. Interpretation ensures that deviance in terms of 'meanings' transpires between persons and the truth or essence of the principle is unpredictable because languge use is not economical. Interpretation is inevitably also a function of experience. Thus 'facts' are not obvious.

Many post-modernists would declare that truth lies at the intersection of interpretations and that the search for an objective reality is, in essence, a contradiction. Daily contact with schools and teachers indicates the diversity of systems established to satisfy the legal requirements of the 1981 Act as they are understood by teachers. Diverse systems, diverse procedures, when taken as operational statements of interpretations, create an image of a system which in some respects may be deemed to have lost its way. If the 1981 Act has, for many teachers, become synonymous with due process requirements, if 'special' conjures the image of the 2% rather than the 20%, if social ecological factors dominate in teacher's causal explanations of underachievement, if there is a preoccupation with the disposition of 'support' to the detriment of its dynamical quality, is not all of this attributable to the complex language games played by different parts of the whole? Is there any reason to suppose that reconceptualizing special educational needs would, in principle, provide a better deal for all children? Is it not more profitable to continue to focus on the one question at the heart of each teacher's professional life? How can I help *this* child to learn what society dictates it is desirable s/he should try to learn?

References

Audit Commision/HMI (1992) *Getting in on the Act: provision for pupils with special educational needs: the national picture*. London: DFE, HMSO.

Bernstein, B. (1970) Education can not compensate for Society. *New Society*, **387**, 344–7.

Bronfenbrenner, U. (1979) *The Ecology of Human Development: Experiments by nature and design*. Camb., MA: Harvard University Press.

Burt, C. (1937) *The Backward Child*. London: University of London Press.

Campbell, M. (1986) *The 1981 Education Act: aspects of content and implementation*. London: DES.

Centre for Studies on Integration in Education (1991) *Increases in Segregation*. London: CSIE Press Release.

Conway, A. (1989) 'Teachers' explanations for children with learning difficulties: An analysis of written reports'. *Early Child Development and Care*. **53**. 53–62.

154

Croll, P. and Moses, D. (1985) *One in Five*. London: Routledge and Kegan Paul.

Department of Education and Science (1978) *Special Educational Needs*. (The Warnock Report). London: HMSO.

Edelman, M. (1977) *Political Language: words that succeed and policies that fail*. New York: Academic Press.

Evans, R. (1976) 'The prediction of educational handicap', *Educational Research*. **18**. 2.

Evans, R. and Shaw, D. (1991) 'Concepts and Attributions: issues for resolution in a "whole school" policy on special needs', London: Consultative paper, RIHE.

Evans, R. and Lovey, J. (1992) *Alternative Educational Provision for Years 10 & 11 Pupils excluded from School*. (In press.)

Evans, R., Fry, J., Cawley, M. and Neville-Jones, E. (1992) *An Exploration of Teachers' Conceptions of 'Support'. A multi-level perspective in one London Borough*. (In press.)

Foucault, M. (1977) *Discipline and Punish*. Harmondsworth: Allen Lane.

Gipps, C., Gross, H. and Goldstein, H. (1987) *Warnock's Eighteen Percent*. London: Falmer Press.

Hanko, G. (1989) 'Sharing Expertise: developing the consultative role', in Evans, R. (ed). *Special Educational Needs: Policy and Practice*. Oxford: Basil Blackwell.

Hart, S. (1992) 'Evaluating Support Teaching', in Booth, T., Swann, W., Masterton, M., and Potts, P. (eds) *Curricula for Diversity in Education*. Milton Keynes: Routledge, Open University.

Joseph, Sir Keith. (1985) Keynote Address to NARE Easter Conference, Froebel College, London.

Minuchin, S. (1974) *Families and Family Therapy*. Camb. MA: Harvard University Press.

National Curriculum Council (1989) Curriculum Guidance 2. *'A Curriculum for All'*. York: NCC.

National Curriculum Council (1992) Curriculum Guidance 9. *'The National Curriculum and Pupils with Severe Learning Difficulties'*. York: NCC.

National Curriculum Council. (1992) Curriculum Guidance 10. *'Teaching Science to Pupils with Special Educational Needs'*. York: NCC.

Schön, D. (1987) *Educating the Reflective Practitioner*. London: Josey-Bass.

Wedge, P. and Prosser, H. (1973) *Born to Fail?* London: Arrow Books for the National Children's Bureau.

CHAPTER 14

Special Needs and Effecti[ve] Learning: Towards a Coll[aborative] Model for the Year 2000

Alan Dyson and Charles Gains

A rationale for change

Provision for students with special needs in mainstream schools is in crisis. At a time when almost every part of the education system can fairly claim much the same, why do we regard special needs as being in particularly dire straits? The following occur to us:

- *Conceptually,* the notion of special educational needs, on which practice has been founded for many years, has come to seem increasingly problematic. Although it gives the appearance of defining a group of students and a set of teaching approaches which are somehow different from others, it has come to seem quite impossible to draw the line between 'special' and 'ordinary' in any convincing way.

- *In curricular terms* the idea of 'special or 'alternative' curricula have given way to notions of 'entitlement' and 'access'. However, the National Curriculum to which students with special needs are supposedly entitled is not founded on any discernible notion of what constitutes quality education for all, and the appropriateness of large parts of it to large numbers of students is highly questionable.

- *At school level* the so-called 'whole school approach' has proved far from easy to implement, and there are serious questions to be asked both about the effectiveness of some of its key strategies – such as in-class support – and about the willingness of some mainstream teachers to accept responsibility in any real sense for the education of more problematic students. At the same time, the resources which have sustained the approach are being progressively

...eezed by the combined effects of National Curriculum staffing demands and the local management of schools, while a climate of competition between schools appears to be making special needs students unattractive to some of them. Not surprisingly, therefore, there is growing evidence of a significant increase in numbers of students excluded from schools, or for whom statements are being sought.

- *At local level* the ability of local authorities to manage a 'continuum of provision' has been seriously eroded. On the one hand, they have declining resources with which to respond to the rising tide of exclusions and referrals, and on the other their ability to manage provision in mainstream schools by deploying specialist teachers, maintaining support services and establishing mainstream 'units' is rapidly diminishing. At the same time, the notion of the 'all-inclusive' neighbourhood school, managed by the local education authority on behalf of the community, has been called into serious question by the increased diversification of schools through open enrolment, opting out, the establishment of city technology colleges (CTCs) and the encouragement in some areas of so-called 'magnet' schools.

It is tempting to see such a catalogue of difficulties as random coincidences, or, at most, a collision between the liberal ideology of special educators and the priorities of a right-wing government. Our own analysis is somewhat different. We contend that:

Underlying the current crisis lies a shift in thinking at a fundamental level.

That shift is taking place before its implications are fully understood, with the consequence that we are left with a special needs edifice from beneath which the ground has been removed. It is not enough, therefore, to hold firm to our established practice for as long as we can, in the hope that the political climate will change. Rather, we need to understand a shift in which we are all involved and which is deeper than the policies of a particular government, so that we can base our future practice on the new focus which is emerging.

A shift of focus

What, then, is this fundamental shift? We believe that, put simply:

> **Educational thinking is moving from a focus on structures to a focus on processes.**

Traditionally in education – and, indeed, in many areas of management – there has been a technical-rational approach to problematic situations. That is, problems have been seen not as unique but as occurring in predictable patterns; it follows that solutions can be created prior to the occurrence of any specific problematic situation. In other words, solutions can be *structured* in advance and specific problems simply have to be shunted towards the appropriate structural solution. All that is required is some centralized managing agency to identify likely problems, devise and resource the appropriate structures and 'shunt' specific problems.

The diversity of students, for instance, tends to be problematic for teachers and schools. Our solutions to this problem have been largely structural – the creating of different sorts of schools, classes, curricula and teaching styles. Within the field of special needs in particular, we have been very strong on creating special schools, special classes, remedial groups, support services, specialist teachers, specialist teaching programmes – all structural solutions to a supposedly predictable pattern of need.

However, we detect rapidly declining confidence in the subtlety and effectiveness of this structural approach. There is a move away from concern with the *pattern* of problems towards an interest in the *unique features* of each problematic situation. Problems are best solved – so the emerging focus suggests – not by setting up structures to anticipate them, but by examining and reconstructing the *processes* out of which they arise. And since this cannot be done centrally or in advance, problem-solving becomes both the responsibility and the *modus operandi* of the practitioner 'on the ground'. The role of any central authority, therefore, is no more than to set a broad framework of control and support within which practitioners may operate.

This sort of thinking seems to underlie the substantial transfer of power in recent years from local education authorities to schools. Individual schools, so the argument goes, need to be free to fulfil their own purposes in response to their own situations, unhampered by the remote bureaucracy of the local authority with its rigid structures and predetermined responses. Similarly, the National Curriculum, for all that it prescribes a broad framework, also assumes that teachers and schools will operate as problem-solvers in interpreting that framework for their own students. Such an overarching framework, sheltering a multiplicity of problem-solving initiatives is, the thinking seems to be, greatly preferable to a series of tightly-prescribed 'alternative' curricula, each one intended for a different category of student.

From these examples, it may be possible to tease out the sorts of dimensions along which forms of educational provision derived from these foci are likely to differ:

Figure 1 Contrasting dimensions of educational provision

Traditional	Emerging
Problem-shunting	Problem-solving
Centralized	Devolved
Structure-focused	Process-focused
Rigidly patterned	Flexible and responsive within broad central control
Categorizing	Differentiating
Defining specialist roles	Encouraging skills interchange
Hierarchical	Networking

This leads us back to special needs in mainstream schools and to the current crisis. Much recent work, in terms of the whole-school approach, differentiation, curriculum access and so on, clearly owes something to the idea of process-oriented problem solving by mainstream teachers as the principal strategy for meeting student diversity.

However, the continued distinctions between 'special' and 'ordinary' needs, the continued existence of special needs teachers, of special needs departments in schools and of centralized local authority provision outside mainstream schools, together with the continued location of ultimate responsibility for special needs provision outside the mainstream are all based on the earlier way of thinking. The trouble is that the two views are mutually incompatible; they effectively sabotage one another.

We wish to suggest, therefore, that it is a failure fully to understand and embrace the emerging focus which is the major source of the current crisis. If we are to resolve that crisis, it is imperative that we carry the debate into new territory, radically rethinking both the notion of special needs and the way in which provision is constructed and managed.

Rethinking special needs

The notion of special needs derives from the traditional focus. For all its individualization, it is actually about categorizing students as 'special' or 'ordinary', about identifying the relatively stable characteristics of the 'special' students (their 'needs'), and about allocating those students to the appropriate structural solution of the problems they present — even if these solutions do follow them, in the shape of support teachers, into the mainstream classroom. The concept of 'individual differences', currently growing in popularity as an alternative to 'special needs', is equally tradition-bound. It still implies that diversity demands different structures for different students and that what matters, therefore, are the stable characteristics of students which distinguish them one from another. It is not, we would suggest, the way forward.

What we need is a language which allows us to adopt a problem-solving, process-focused stance. Since the key process which is the *raison d'être* of schools is the process of learning, then key concepts for thinking about schools must be to do with that process. Accordingly we propose the following terms as means of helping us to conceptualize differently the field which we currently call 'special needs':

- **Effective learning** — a notional ideal process which schools and teachers strive to generate and sustain for their students; and
- **Learning breakdown** — what happens when that ideal process is not sustained.

However, we emphatically do *not* see effective learning as what happens for most students and learning breakdown as what happens for some. On the contrary, because learning is, by definition, about working at the limits, it is also about finding those limits, testing them, and sometimes going too far beyond them. Therefore we would argue that:

- **Learning breakdown is endemic in the learning process for** *all* **students**
- **Teaching is a problem-solving process to do with maximizing learning effectiveness.** It involves on the one hand being proactive in creating situations in which learning is likely, and on the other being responsive towards the breakdown of those situations.

Language such as this still allows us to talk about students failing to learn, about teachers failing to teach, and about why some students in some situations seem particulary difficult to teach effectively. But it does so without drawing distinctions between categories of student, or inviting us to allocate different students to different programmes, teachers or schools. What we now call 'special needs' becomes indistinguishable from the 'normal' and complex process of teaching and learning for all.

Managing provision for effective learning

Unfortuately, the literature on 'special needs' is full of definitions and redefinitions, many of which have remained at the level of rhetoric. The question that arises, therefore, is whether it is possible to describe forms of provision and practice which would make our reconceptualization a reality.

We would argue that implicit in our initial characterization of emerging educational systems are three fundamental components of such provision:

- *Autonomous providers* – teachers and schools with devolved powers and resources responding as problem-solvers to their own situations
- *Strategic control* – some management system beyond the individual teacher and individual school, charged with setting the parameters of the problems to be solved, with devolving

responsibilities and resources, and with monitoring outcomes
- *Networks and interactions* – mechanisms whereby individual providers enhance their ability to solve problems by interchanging skills and resources, by collaborating for mutual benefit, or, in some cases, by aggressively stripping each other's assets.

These components are, we would suggest, already clearly visible in the relationships between schools and local authorities generated by local management of schools (LMS). However, special needs provision, perhaps more than any other branch of education, has been dominated by the tradition of structural solutions managed and resourced from the centre by special needs departments internally and by local education authorities externally. What, therefore, do these components look like when applied to this field?

A collaborative model

Figure 2 presents a model of what provision *might* look like if current trends were continued and, crucially, if the implications of the shift we have described were fully understood and acted upon. Granted the confusion and uncertainty which surrounds policy making at all levels, this is not so much an attempt to predict how the future *will* be, therefore, as to indicate how the future realistically *might* be if decision-makers at all levels of the system choose this way forward. Whilst we are not prepared to say unequivocally that 'there is no alternative', we would suggest that all the alternatives we can imagine look considerably less attractive.

The model posits autonomous schools working within a framework set by what we have called an enabling structure. It envisages schools collaborating together in clusters and making joint use of support and development services. It further envisages clusters collaborating together in consortia and making use of core services, provided by external agencies or commissioned by the enabling structure. Although the model illustrates how current roles and functions could be redistributed, it aims to do much more than that. It is an attempt to show how the notion of schools as problem-solving organizations, striving to create the conditions for effective learning, can give rise to a working educational system.

We now propose to analyse the components of the model in some detail.

162

Figure 2 A collaborative model for the provision of services to students with 'special needs'

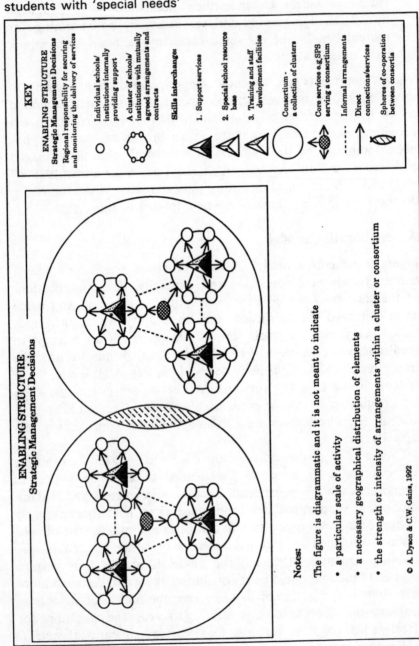

The enabling structure

Whereas the role of the local authority (or special needs department at school level) has traditionally been to make and manage provision that was not made by the mainstream, the role of the enabling structure is precisely to enable; that is to create conditions under which the mainstream *can* make effective provision. It therefore has three tasks:

- to set parameters within which mainstream schools operate, in particular by devolving to them a clearly-defined set of educational responsibilities
- to devolve resources and powers appropriate to the discharge of those responsibilities
- to monitor the effectiveness of schools in discharging their responsibilities and to take control action where necessary

Setting parameters. The responsibility for providing education for given students has traditionally rested with the local education authority. Mainstream schools have, quite literally, been irresponsible; they have been one amongst a number of local authority maintained structures, and they have been designed and resourced to provide educational services for only a proportion of the student population.

The model proposes a major transfer of responsibility to mainstream schools, together with a concomitant transfer of resources and powers. The mechanism for such a transfer could be the delineation of catchment areas, but is more likely to be parental choice – in line with the ideas of a Parents' Charter, and in the light of the current denial of choice to parents of statemented students. There are, however, two caveats:

- The school's responsibility will not necessarily be to *provide* education from within its own teaching resources, but *to secure education by deploying its financial resources* (see below)
- The enabling structure may, therefore, decide to withhold responsibility for a small number of highly atypical students, not on the grounds that mainstream schools cannot educate them, but that they cannot efficiently and effectively *secure* educaton for them.

Accordingly the model envisages virtually all students becoming the responsibility of mainstream schools, with the enabling structure providing or commissioning only certain forms of strategic provision for such groups as deaf-blind students or students with severe emotional and behavioural difficulties. Moreover, this distinction is a pragmatic, not an educational or philosophical one, and wherever the line is drawn, it will be both necessary and possible to set clear and unequivocal criteria.

Devolving resources. Current mechanisms for allocating resources in respect of special needs rest on the assumption that detailed description of a student's characteristics ('needs') make it possible to delineate appropriate provision and, therefore, to allocate appropriate resources. We contest each step in this chain, arguing that the real task is to give the school an adequate resource-base from which to problem-solve in respect of its more problematical students. That is precisely the same task as for all other students.

This, we believe, can be achieved in the following way:

- for the large majority of students individual assessment is not necessary because the resource needs generated by such students are recurrent and predictable. Formula funding with weightings based on whole school population surveys is all that is needed
- there will be a small minority of students whose education has clear resource implications but whose presence in a school population is neither recurrent nor predictable. The resource (rather than educational) needs of these students will have to be assessed − but this need be no more complex than allocating them to a resource band by means of pre-determined criteria.

The model does not, therefore, envisage the need for a statementing procedure in its current form. Educational assessment for problematical students, as for all others, is only loosely linked to resource assessment and is essentially a matter for schools, not for administrators.

Monitoring outcomes. The devolution of responsibility and resources to schools, together with the disappearance of direct local authority prescription and management of provision, makes the effective monitoring of outcomes a major priority for the enabling structure. The model envisages this taking place in two ways:

- *Lay accountability.* Schools are accountable to the community in general, and to parents and students in particular, for securing high-quality education. This accountability is delivered by means of the governing body, parental choice, strengthened parental rights of complaint, and, perhaps, formal contracting between schools and parents

- *Professional accountability.* Schools are accountable to the education system as a whole through processes of inspection. This implies that the inspection process will need a strong focus on problematical students and will need to be frequent and detailed enough to follow up on individual cases. Current proposals in this respect may not be adequate to this task.

Thus, in this monitoring capacity, the enabling structure becomes the guardian and advocate both of the student's and parents' rights and of notional values and priorities. Although there is a tension in this role, it perhaps is less than that experienced by local authorities as both providers and inspectors.

The form of the enabling structure. The model deliberately employs a non-specific term such as 'enabling structure' to designate a role rather than a particular organization. This role could be fulfilled by reconstructed local education authorities, or district councils, or regional bodies, or the Department For Education, or (to some extent) by market forces, or by some combination of these. Certainly a non-unitary structure might ease the tension alluded to above. Whatever the form of this enabling structure, however, two characteristics are essential:

- that the *whole* of the role described above is discharged in some way and
- that the enabling structure is itself effectively accountable to the individuals and community on whose behalf it acts.

Mainstream schools and clusters

The model sees mainstream schools as the autonomous, *but not isolated,* securers of educaton for the vast majority of students. We contend that the traditional focus, with its emphasis on structural solutions, has led educationalists to think in terms of simple dichotomies: mainstream *versus* special, integration *versus* segregation. It has also led to the currently fashionable view that mainstream schools ought to be able to 'consume their own smoke' if only they would organize themselves appropriately.

We believe that:

> Such simplistic notions disappear if we view schools, not as a structures for providing a particular type of education, but as **the locus of a range of educational services whereby effective learning is secured for all students within a flexibly-organized system.**

The model envisages mainstream schools wishing and being able to provide most of these services from within their own teaching resources. However, they will also need to reach beyond themselves for externally-provided services. Some of these will come from individually-negotiated contracts with freelance agencies (perhaps reconstructed local authority support and psychological services). Many, however, will arise from collaborations with other schools in cluster groups. A cluster in this sense is any grouping of schools which comes together for mutual benefit. Although schools may not be compelled to cluster, and although there are currently pressures of competition to drive them apart, there are also powerful reasons for a collaborative approach. This would, for instance, allow schools to:

- pool resources in order to achieve economies of scale (e.g. by employing their own specialist teachers)
- develop specialisms within individual schools and operate a skills-interchange across the cluster, thus offering parents and students access to a broad range of services from any school base
- negotiate with outside agencies, services and other clusters from a position of strength.

It is not necessary or even desirable for there to be a single, centrally-directed pattern of clusters. Schools will come together in different ways for different purposes, and clusters may be permanent or temporary, formal or informal, geographical or pyramidal or otherwise. Nonetheless,

> **We envisage fairly stable structures emerging in order to meet predictable and recurrent demands which individual schools would otherwise find difficult to meet from their own teaching resources.**

Hence, clusters might wish to employ their own behaviour support teachers, or share the expertise of an effective learning co-ordinator, or develop a specific learning difficulties resource base in one particular school.

Where demands are less recurrent or where provision is too costly for clusters to maintain in-house, the model sees such clusters collaborating together as consortia, which will maintain their own specialist services, or buy them from self-managing agencies, or make use of core services commissioned by the enabling structure. The precise nature of the pattern of services will vary from area to area, but this is an example of the sort of hierarchy that might emerge:

Individual school – subject specialist, in-class support teachers

Cluster – shared effective learning co-ordinator, specialist support teachers, shared access to specific learning difficulties centre in one school and vocationally-oriented post-14 provision in another

Consortium – peripatetic visual and auditory impairment service, and access to psychological service, special school/base provision maintained/commissioned as core services by enabling structure.

In order to manage this system we see clusters and consortia maintaining a minimal administrative structure, which would effectively consist of a skills interchange, identifying demand, auditing available skills and resources, and arranging for students and teachers to access them. There would need within this structure to be some form of accountancy procedure – a pooling of resources might be simpler than an item-by-item account. There would also be a need and opportunity to make parental choice in effect not choice of a school in isolation, but of a school as part of a cluster. This would both damp down some of the more destructive effects of competition and circumvent the problem of parents choosing schools not resourced to meet their children's specific needs.

Implications

It is our view that the model we have outlined is not only desirable but is, in some form or another, likely to emerge from the current confusion. We now wish to examine, therefore, what the implications of this emergence will be for various parts of the education service, and how they could begin to respond.

Implications for mainstream schools

Mainstream schools will need to rethink fundamentally their roles. They will no longer be providers of limited forms of education to limited categories of student, within a much larger structure managed for them by the local education authority. Rather they will be self-managing securers of effective learning for virtually all students. They will, therefore, need to:

● audit their existing skills and resources to determine what services they can provide in-house
● begin exploring collaborative partnerships with other schools and services in order to supplement what they can provide internally
● identify opportunities to develop specialist skills and resources which can be marketed to the cluster and consortium.

They will also, if they are not to become heavily dependent on (and therefore indebted to) external services, need to look at how they can develop their internal capacity for sustaining effective learning. In order to do this, they will have to replicate the components of the model internally. This means that they will have to:

● devolve responsibilities, resources and powers to departments, teams and individual teachers
● make those responsibilities wide-ranging but clear
● ensure that teachers and departments are accountable for the discharge of those responsibilities.

Above all, we suggest that:

Schools will have to organize themselves internally so that each classroom, like each school, is the locus of a range of educational services flexibly delivered, which secure effective learning for all students.

Organization in terms of isolated classrooms shunting problems into a special needs system is no more appropriate within the school than it is beyond the school.

There is much that could be said about how this might be achieved. It may be sufficient to highlight three points:

● there are already examples of responsive means of organizing support for learning beginning to emerge in schools. Such examples – flexible learning would be the most obvious one – tend to stress the opening up of the classrooms to other teachers and adults, to a range of learning resources, and to a range of teaching approaches

- flexible organization is crucially dependent for its success on genuine collaboration between teachers. Moves to break down professional isolation by means of collegial and team approaches, joint problem-solving and internal consultancy are likely to be as important to development within schools as clustering is to development between schools

- schools basing themselves on the problem-solving model advocated here will depend heavily on high-quality information on the nature of problems and on their success in solving them. Very few schools currently have such information; it will be essential to generate this, not simply for purposes of accountability, but in order to facilitate organizational and professional development.

Implications for 'special needs' teachers

Special needs teachers, just as much as schools, will need to rethink their roles. As a form of structural solution to special needs problems, their mere presence in schools, almost as an extra pair of hands, has often been enough. There has been no pressing need to clarify what, precisely, they could contribute to effective learning for all students. The model we are proposing, with its emphasis on problem solving by mainstream teachers supported by a range of flexibly-delivered services, requires special needs teachers to clarify what are the services they can offer and how they can support the problem-solving process.

We envisage two directions in which such clarification can proceed:

Increasing specialization

Some special needs teachers will develop or clarify genuinely specialized skills which will enable them to make a distinctive contribution to their school and which will be marketable within their cluster and consortium. *Real* expertise in reading difficulties, specific learning difficulties, counselling, thinking skills, behaviour management, or 'alternative' teaching strategies is as necessary as real expertise in curriculum areas, information technology, staff development or the management of delegated budgets. Not every teacher has – or can be expected to have – such expertise, and therefore it constitutes a valuable commodity which does not simply replicate 'good teaching'.

Increasing generalization

Other special needs teachers may move in what, in some senses, is the opposite direction, away from the development of highly specialized teaching skills towards the ability to contribute to the whole-school management of effective learning provision. This would demand involvement in a whole range of issues beyond those traditionally regarded as forming the special needs remit. It would also require a high level of skill in two areas:

- organizational development and the management of change
- staff development and the management of personnel.

    Such 'generalizing' teachers would thus effectively become part of the school's senior management team and would no longer be identified with problematical students alone.

Implications for local authority support services, psychological services and special schools

The model suggests that the traditional role of these local authority agencies will largely cease to exist, and they, like special needs teachers, will be required either to define a new role or to disappear. However, the model also indicates that a new role is available as part of a range of services in a flexible system. This new role requires these agencies to:

- define the *distinctive contribution* they can make which schools and clusters cannot make
- market that contribution to schools by helping them to understand its value.

We would contend that many such agencies currently make a contribution that is either not sufficiently distinctive or is not valued by schools. However, there are a number of areas of considerable potential:

- highly specialized expertise which schools and clusters cannot develop efficiently (in, for instance, hearing impairment or the education of traveller children)
- flexible (fixed-term or part-time) placements on specialised programmes (e.g. vocationally-oriented curricula at 14 +)

- consultancy and development work with teachers and schools.

A shift away from the shunting of special needs problems towards structural solutions has two effects. On the one hand it deprives these agencies of their guaranteed workload and livelihood. On the other, it offers them the opportunity to be proactive in contributing to schools' problem-solving. For special schools in particular there are opportunities to develop Warnock's resource centre idea in a way that has not been possible so long as they have been seen simply as sidings into which special needs problems disappear.

Implications for local education authorities

At the time of writing, everything is uncertain about the role of local authorities except that it will continue to change. Our model nonetheless suggests that there are specific moves which local authorities can make in order to ensure that change is more rather than less productive. Indeed, we would argue that these are steps that some local authorities have been taking for some time with positive results:

- local authorities will need to define clearly for schools what their responsibilities are in respect of problematical students, and which responsibilities pass at which points back to the authority
- they will need to delegate resources and powers which make it possible for schools to discharge their responsibilities
- they will need to facilitate the development in schools of problem-solving approaches to such students
- they will need to work with schools to develop clear and explicit systems of accountability based on high-quality information
- they will need to enable and encourage schools to collaborate in clusters and consortia.

Implications for the Government

Within this model, the Government is the ultimate 'enabling structure'. This role demands a 'hands-off' management approach which has been one theme, at least, of Government policy since 1979. However, it also demands a very 'hands-on' approach to protecting the educational entitlement of problematical and vulnerable students. We are not proposing a system driven by free-market competition, but one in which devolved responsibilities are closely monitored on the basis of advocacy and guardianship of students' rights. The principal implication for Government, therefore, is that a legislative framework is needed which defines clearly the entitlement of students, the responsibilities of schools, and the procedures for enforcing those responsibilities and guaranteeing those rights.

Rethinking special needs: towards the year 2000

This chapter has been an attempt to rethink the form of what we now call special needs provision from fundamental principles. Much of the detail of how such a system might look in practice cannot, because it is a responsive problem-solving system, be specified in advance. Much else we have been compelled to omit for reasons of space and clarity. We believe that there is considerable supportive evidence for our ideas, that other writers have detected similar movements, and that elements of our model are already emerging on the ground. Above all, we wish to acknowledge an enormous debt to the other contributors to this volume, whose detailed analyses have emboldened us to piece together something which we hope makes a coherent whole.

There is considerable opportunity, we believe, for the reader to question, amplify, modify or reject our ideas. We see this as an advantage rather than a problem. The edifice of special needs provision as we know it is unlikely to survive the year 2000. Radical rethinking is urgently needed. If this contribution engages others in such a process, and if that process results in a more coherent, effective and, ultimately, just system of provision, then it will have served its purpose.

Index

Warnock Report (1978) x, 49, 64,
    67–8, 70, 101, 123, 142, 146,
    150, 151, 152, 171
Weltanshauung 13, 18
William Howard School 77–8

withdrawal *see* selective teaching

Youth Training Schemes 58–9
youth village **57–63**